THE TABLETS

Armand Schwerner

THE TABLETS

THE NATIONAL POETRY FOUNDATION

ORONO, MAINE 1999

Copyright © 1968, 1971, 1975, 1976, 1983, 1985, 1988, 1989, 1999, Estate of Armand Schwerner.

05 04 03 02 01 00 99   1 2 3 4 5

Published by The National Poetry Foundation, University of Maine, Orono, Maine 04469-5752.
Printed by Cushing-Malloy, Inc., Ann Arbor, Michigan 48107. Distributed by University Press
of New England, Hanover and London.

Design: Michael Alpert and Betsy Rose. Cover photo: Phill Niblock.

The paper used in this publication meets the minimum requirements of the American National
Standard for Information Sciences—Permanence of Paper for Printed Library Materials, ansi
z39.48-1984.

The publication of this book was made possible in part by a grant from the Stephen and Tabitha
King Foundation. The National Poetry Foundation wishes to acknowledge the help of Michael
Heller in the production of this book. The NPF also thanks Michael Bergstein of *Conjunctions*.

The Tablets were previously published or taped as follows: *The Tablets I-VIII*, West Branch, Iowa:
Cummington Press, 1968; *The Tablets I-XV*, New York: Grossman, 1971; *The Tablets I-XVIII* (tape
edition), Hattingen, West Germany: S-Press, 1974; *Tablets XVI, XVII, XVIII*, Deerfield, Massa-
chusetts: Heron Press, 1975; *This Practice, Tablet XIX and Other Poems*, London: Permanent Press,
1976; *Tablets XV, XVI, XVII, XVIII* (tape edition),. New York: New Wilderness Audiographics #
7708A, 1977; *Sounds of the River Naranjana and The Tablets I-XXIV*, Barrytown, NY: Station Hill
Press, 1983; "Tablet XXV," NY: *Conjunctions*, Winter 1985; "Tablet XXVI, Laboratory-Teachings-
Memoirs of the Scholar/Translator," NY: *Conjunctions*, Summer 1988; *The Tablets I-XXVI*,
London: Atlas Press, 1989; "Tablet XXVII," *Conjunctions* 1991.

Library of Congress Cataloging-in-Publication Data

   Schwerner, Armand.
      The tablets / Armand Schwerner.
         p.   cm.
      Contents: Tablets I-XXVII.
      ISBN 0-943373-55-7 (cloth).— ISBN 0-943373-56-5 (pbk.)
      I. Title.
   PS3569.C57T26   1999
   811'.54--dc21   99-21937
                                                       CIP

CONTENTS

KEY TO SYMBOLS

. . . . untranslatable
+ + + + + + missing
(?) variant reading
[ ] supplied by the scholar translator

THE TABLETS

TABLET I

All that's left is pattern* (shoes?).

> *doubtful reconstruction

I rooted about . . . like a . . . . sow* for her pleasure

> *atavism: a hieroglyph; perhaps 'a fetal pig,' 'a small pig,' 'goddess'

the (power)* for all of [us] !

> *perhaps 'damage,' if a borrowing; cf. cognate in N. Akkadian: 'skin-burn'

I made a mistake. The small path was barely muddy. Little squush;
           and wet socks.* It is (scholarship?) (meditation?)

> *modernism. Specificity of attire a problem. Possibly 'underwear'
(dryness?)

and the . . . . (energy?) the (energy?) the (pig?)* of the [mistake] ! . . . . .
           (energy?) . . . .

> *hieroglyph again: 'god' may be meant here

war/good-ness . . . ./cunt* (thresher?)/marvel/cunt*/bright-yellow/
           bright-ochre†/bright-bright-yellow/bright-ochre-yellow/
           bright-yellow-yellow-yellow-ochre-yellow ‡ §

> *hieroglyph, probably not syllabic. Very old ▓ : conceivably haloed by
hair—but rake-like, very much the rake in the Kap-Kol-Bak-Silpotli-Wap frieze
in the young consort's left hand. (See Ouspenskaya: *The Young Consort and the Rake
Muckery,* Egypt. Annals, Surah P, P, iii.)
>   † see Halevy-Cohen, *The Prismatic Function in Early Man: a study in
Imperceptible Gradations*, U. U. Press, Ak., 1922–1962
>   ‡ analogue of segmented compass readings? as NE, NNE, etc. We know
the god Pri-Prik usually assumed yellow guises in his search for the eighteen-fold
path. See Marduk, *The Babylonians,* Hirsute VII, Liber A-413, Tigris.
>   § The entire sequence is a rare example of restriction of categories in one
'line' or 'cadence' or 'unit' or 'verset.' Only nominal forms used.

13

[handwritten annotation:] In format this is identical to an actual scholarly journal but the content is hysterical. Maintains a professional, scholarly tone.

the emptying of yellow

+ + + + + + + + + + +
+ + + + + + + + + + + + + + + +
+ + + + +
+ + + + +
+ + + + +
he calls himself 'with grey horses'
he is 'having fine green oxen'
with (purpose?) + + + + + + + + + + in the dream (nightmare?)
+ + + + + + + + + + + + + + + + of a sharp blade
[testicles] . . . . for the ground
shit (sweat?) upon the . . . .
rain upon the . . . .
saliva upon the . . . .
heart's blood upon the . . . .
children's strange (beautiful?) early blood in the . . . . . .
. . . . from the old dryness (underwear?)
vomit (yellow?/north?) does not slake ground
pus (ochre?/NNE?) does not stanch the wounds in the ground
bile (yellow-ochre?/NNNE?) does not + + + + + + + + + +
he is splayed on the . . . . like a worn-out pig (god?)
he is un- + + + + + + + +
he is dis- + + + + + + + + + + + +
he is + + + + + + + + + + + -less
he is de- + + + + + + + + + + +
he is impossible on the dry ground + + + + + + + + + before . . . .
he is non- + + + + + + + +
he is pre- + + + + + + + + + +*

*the isolated prefix remnants are curious. The tablet seems rubbed out with care. Is this segment an early attempt to unite form and meaning? graphic as well as substantial emptiness?

the ants look (scrounge?) for food
the ground-pig (lower god?) sucks dry filth for water
the palaces are yellow (vomit?/N?)
look at the fishermen in their patterns (shoes?) !
they count the directions of emptiness by fish-names
N shad
E cod
S mackerel
W tuna
from the shad no rain weighs on the breeze
from the cod the loud wind is dry (unforgiving?)*

*interesting. We find ourselves at or near the very point in time where the word, concrete in origin, shades off into an abstraction.

hanging-mackerel-tail-up-smoke-death*

*virtually untranslatable. This is an attempt at an Indo-European nominalization of *kili-pap-swad-ur-plonz*. We can convey little of the conceptual category 'fish-death,' rather 'up-down-fish-dying-becoming' which refers in a coterminous visionary metaphysic to both time-bound organisms (like the urus, say) and the Death God, *plonz,* in his timeless brooding.

the tuna is mighty the tuna is mighty the way of up-down, smoke-death
the men dance around the stone
the stones dance over the pit
the pits dance beyond the bodies like the air-hog (god of low rain-clouds?)
the bodies the bodies the bodies the bodies the bodies the bodies
beyond the bodies the trees dance
the bodies need to fuck the trees
the dry (unforgiving?) bodies wait twenty-eight days
the blood of the four bodies shad
the blood of the four bodies cod
the blood of the four bodies mackerel
the blood of the four bodies tuna*

*four bodies here; six of them in the previous mention. Odd. — rituals wherein people attempt to control the weather (?)

they will change the bile
they will change the cold pus unless . . . . . . because . . . . fish-death
they will-would-might-have-can-change* the winter of NNE

*tense untranslatable; outside Indo-European categories

do they destroy the ochre, the shad/shad-cod? do they eat?
they wait for the fat pig (god?)
+ + + + + + + + + + +
+ + + + + + + + + + + + + +
+ + + + + + + + + +
+ + + + + + + + + + + + + + + + + + +
+ + + + + + +
+ + + + + + + + +
+ +
. . . . of the great Ones (One?)*

*capitalization clearly indicated. The number is in doubt. Is this the pig, or an incredible presage of the early Elohim?

```
+ + + + + + +
+ + + + + + + + + + + +
+ + + + + + + + + pattern (shoes?) . . . . . . . . . . . . . . . . . . . . . . .
+ + + + + + + + + +
+ + + + + + +
+ + + + + + + + + + + + + +
+ + + + + + + + + . . . . . . . . . . . . .
```

TABLET II

This tablet consists of a numbered list. At least a few of the units may be titles to chants which have never been found, or which may have never been written. Its exact placement in the context of the series is a problem.

1. <u>empty</u> holes in the fish-dying-becoming directions
2. . . . . strings and pieces + + + + + + + + +
3. the children dance* in waters of fish-death

      *the idiosyncratic placement of the central horizontal cuneiform wedges suggests the word may be 'breathe.'

4. they are dry scales + + + + + + + + + + + + + + +
5. on the inside their scales are wet (moist?)
6. they are empty holes; why do they walk and walk?
7. the + + + + + + children eat . . . . strings and pieces
8. the <u>empty children run in [their] patterns (shoes</u>?)
9. the pig (god?) waits . . . . fish-death
10. the children . . . .
11. the children . . . . ball games
12. the children . . . .
13. . . . . must eat (might-could-will-want-to-eat?) rain pintrpnit*

      *transliteration. Probably an archaic form of 'alleluiah' or 'selah.'

14. the road . . . . penis-thinking pintrpnit
15. sometimes they walk on the river-road with crocodile pintrpnit
16. they can walk near the knom* in their stupid ignorance of fish-death

      *conceivably 'the Spirit which denies'

17. o they are stupid they are lacking they walk and walk
18. they separate fish and death
19. they do not separate fish and death
20. near the knom they tame the <u>auroch</u> pintrpnit
21. not far from the knom, on spring nights, they tame the urus pintrpnit
22. in stupid ignorance in stupid ignorance how do they walk and walk?
23. in walking the river road they tame wisent* pintrpnit

— some words are carefully explicated while others are left mysterious by the scholar / translator

*auroch, wisent, urus: large long-horned ancestor of the modern bull

24. they are taller than urus pintrpnit
25. how small they are beside the urus pintrpnit
26. the . . . . to suck the rain
27. . . . . .very warm on our knees
28. the long men* + + + + + + + + + + + + to eat the children

*possibly 'priests'

29. not merely to eat, but the blood . . . .
30. not merely to eat but the knom . . . .
31. + + + + + + + + + + + + + + + + + forever
32. brains and liver . . . . many favors
33. the sun/the sun/the sun/the (power?)* for all of [us] !

*possibly 'damage'

34. we have made no mistake/the (energy?)/the (energy?)
35. the sun sits in the [testicles] of the pig (god?)
36. the sun +
37. the long house + + + + + + yellow (N?/shad?/vomit?)
38. the sun from the cod
39. the sun from the cod
40. the sun from the cod
41. the sun from the cod
42. the sun from the cod pintrpnit

TABLET III

Draining of life (handwritten)
sickness, death, decay (handwritten)

the further emptying

the calyx, the calyx, someone has ripped it
it will not make loam, it will crumble
the pig (god?) has pulled life off + + + + + + + +
the pig (god?) is stronger than a thoughtless child
my chest empties . . . . my chest
I can no longer stand in the middle of the field and + + + + + + + +
I am missing, my chest has no food for the maggots
there is no place for the pollen, there is only a hole in the flower
the hummingbird . . . . pus . . . . nectar
the field is a hole without pattern (shoes?)
there are no eyes in the back of the wisent's sockets
the urus eats her own teats and her . . . .
the urus lies in milk and blood
the urus is a hole in the middle of the field
[testicles] . . . . for the ground
'with grey horses' drinks urine
'having fine green oxen' looks for salt
let us hold . . . . the long man upside down
let us look into his mouth . . . . selfish saliva
let us pluck + + + + + + + + + + + + + for brother tree
let us kiss the long man, let us carry the long man
let us kiss the long man, let us fondle the long man
let us carry the long man as the ground sucks his drippings
let us feel the drippings from his open groin
let us kiss the hot wound, the wet wound . . . . nectar
let us wait until he is white and dry . . . . my chest
let us look into his dry evil mouth, let us fondle the long man
let us bypass the wisent on the river-road pintrpnit
let us avoid the urus on the river-road pintrpnit
let us smell the auroch on the river-road pintrpnit
let us carry the beautiful (strange?) children to the knom
let us sing with the children by the knom
let us set the children's beautiful (strange?) skulls by the hearth
when the rain comes.
let us have rain

pretty shockingly explicit (handwritten)

19

let us have rain

+ + + + + + + + +

+ + + + + + + + + + +

+ + + + ... tremble

and also to make the strangers piss in their pants for fear

and to make all the neighbors know of the terrible . . . . . that is ours

let them hear about it, let them know

let them tremble like a spear going through the heart and through the back

let them become a knowing spear, let them bore in, fish-death

let them shake from the spear's blow, let them hear it sing

I need to feel my solid arm, I need to feel my mighty penis

o my son at the other edge of fish-death

o my son by the dark river-road I can't reach your fingertips

o my son in the rain your liver will make the barley shoot up

o my son in the rain your eyes will see the way in the wheat

o my son on the happy edge of the emptying, fish-death, pintrpnit

o dark dark dark dark dark dark dark dark dark dark

o dark

you will-would-might-have-can, let us have rain

TABLET IV

Most large fragments are the result of horizontal breaks. This Tablet (IV) and the next (V), however, are vertically fractured. The reconstruction of V is almost certainly correct. Doubt lingers about IV. The edges do not meet in three places; otherwise it is a good tight fit. Whether the idiosyncratic continuity derives from accident or design is a problem which only time and further studies and excavations will resolve. Note the caesuras.

is the man a bush on fire?	like one drop of quartz, two cold onyx beads
is the man four-legged and with teeth?	like one piece of petrified wood
is the man a hot woman?	like one hard-finger-bone, one moonlight on iron
is he mud, of solid mud?	in the shape of one clay tablet in frost
is the man a bird?	. . . . like bronze eyes
is the unhappy man on all fours?	in the shape of bronze statues of something wood
is the man all blood, all bile?	like menstrual blood congealed in cold mud
is the woman a fat belly?	like the world, a five-year-old's bloody . . .
is the man sleeping in a god?	like a frog stuffed with small white stones
is the man's head aching?	like . . . . . . empty + + + + + maggots
does the man play with her lips?	like amber + + + + + + + running pus
can the man make himself come	like a . . . . cold onyx beads
can the woman come on top of the man?	. . . . dead trees
when does the man sacrifice his hands?	like sheep draped in cold mud
does the man wipe her belly with sperm?	like stories about ice, about frozen wheat
does the man put good leaves under his testicles?	+ + + + + + + + + of maggots
does the man put his lips on the sheep's udder?	in the shape of a clay tablet in frost
does the man put hand and elbow in his cow's vagina?	like death in blossoms when . . . . .
does he ram his penis into soft earth?	like the death in petrified wood
does he touch his woman's . . . .?	like the death in two cold onyx beads
does the man pray to her vulva for rain?	like stories about ice, about frozen wheat

21

does he lament the sickness in his groin?   like a frog stuffed with small white
                                                                        pebbles
it is night; does he swim in the river?   like sheep draped by cold mud
+ + + + + + + + + + +   like hail
+ + + + + + + + + + + + +   like a leg burning on the pyre
+ + + + + + + + + + + +   like ants, a rotten cadaver, the dead
                                                                        trees

Attributing worth to life forms
(what, really, in the grand scheme does
make a man any better than a fly's wing)

TABLET V

is the man bigger than a fly's wing? — what pleasure!

is he much bigger than a fly's wing? — what pleasure!

is his hard penis ten times a fly's wing? — what pleasure!

is his red penis fifteen times a fly's wing? — what [pleasure]!

is his mighty penis fifty times a fly's wing? — what pleasure!

does his penis vibrate like a fly's wing? — what terrific pleasure!

is his arm four and one half times a strong penis? — . . . . a great arm

is his arm two hundred-twenty-five times a fly's wing? — in the shape of
petrified wood

is his body three times his great arm? — what pleasure!

is his body thirteen times his red penis? — what pleasure!

is his body three-hundred-thirty-six times a big fly's body? — what pleasure!

does he touch his body with pleasure? — what pleasure!

does she count fly's wings throughout the night? — what pleasure!

is her vulva tipped with spring color? — what terrific pleasure!

does he move behind in her? — let us have rain!

does she vibrate like the wheel on the axle? — let us have rain! what pleasure!

let us call a fly's half-wing *kra* — lay a *kra* on this bull's horn

let us call a fly's half-wing *kra* — lay another *kra* on this bull's horn

let us call a fly's half-wing *kra* — lay another *kra* on this bull's horn

let us call a fly's half-wing *kra* — lay another *kra* on this bull's horn

let us call a fly's half-wing *kra* — lay another *kra* on this bull's horn

let us call a fly's half-wing *kra* — hold the bull down quiet

let us call a fly's half-wing *kra* — lay another *kra* on this bull's horn

look, the bull's horn is more than six *kra*! — hold down the bull's head

let us call the man's red penis *pro* — lay a *pro* on this cow's vulva

let us call the man's red penis *pro* — lay another *pro* on this cow's vulva

let us call the man's red penis *pro* — lay another *pro* on this cow's vulva

look, the cow's vulva is five *kra* — what pleasure!

look, the cow's vulva is almost three *pro* — what terrific pleasure!

pro kra kra pro kra kra kra pro — *kra* what pleasure! *pro* what pleasure!

the man's sacrificed hand is more than one *pro* — this twig is more than one *pro*

the man's aching head is forty *kra* round — this great melon is forty *kra* round

the man's sick groin is three *pro* — feel this lamb shank, three *pro*

23

let's sacrifice this twig

let's sacrifice this great melon

let's sacrifice this shank

the hand is furious

the aching head screams

the sick groin is furious

+ + + + + + + + + +

+ + + + + + + + +

+ + + + + + + + + + + +

what a pleasure!

what a pleasure!

what a terrific pleasure!

how will we frighten the strangers now?

how will they piss in their pants?

how will we frighten the strangers now?

+ + + + + + + + + +

+ + + + + + + + + + + + + +

+ + + + + + + for water

Who is the speaker of this preface?

TABLET VI

Here the scholar-translator has tried to approximate the colloquial tone of the original. Unfortunately we have no information about the identity of the addressee; anger and ridicule are directed toward some immanent power which keeps changing its attributes; rough approximations of its being may be embodied in variously found names: Big Fat Flux   Great Hole in the Cock Liver (perhaps a reference to poorly understood onanistic ritual practices directed to the air-hog or the ground-pig)   Sore-Ass-Mole-Face-Snivel-Kra Little Mover   Big Mover Seventeen-Eyeball-Fusion-Up-Up   The One of This Way   The One of That Way   The One of No Way   Anxious-Liar-Fart-Flyaway   The Smeller   The Diggger   The Scheming Pintrpnit   The Porous Poppycock   The Mean-Sucking-Sponge-Pinipnipni   Pnouk   Lak   Pa-Pa-the-Flying-Slime   The Big Eater   The Paramount Groin of the Sucking Air Old No-Name   The Rock   The Fly   The Killer of Water   The Beautiful (Strange?) Liar   The Rain-Spoiler   The Water Dryer   The Tree Dryer   The Flower Dryer   The Urus Dryer   The Creep   The Knom of Lies   The Great Trouble   The Scheming Rock   The Maggot   The Friendly Buzzard Everybody's Hyena   The Dumpy Snivel   The Filthy Teat   The Foosh. It has been suggested that the concrete figures belong to an earlier layer; our knowledge, however, is not at such a point of sophistication that we can now attempt a Higher Criticism of this material. When we can, what germinative cultural possibilities might we not discover?

. . . . in the world. I can't come
you have oozed into my + + + + + + + + + old Water Dryer
+ + + + + + + because when I reach the end of my story, I'll still have
all of it to tell in me waiting to explode
like the constipation in a plugged-up man after . . . .
Big Mover I still can't come, my woman is unhappy with me
she waits but she's getting + + + + + + + + and madder
old Water Dryer you are fat tree-gum and . . . . . . and fungus in my loins
this is not me, o Pa-Pa-the-Flying-Slime, this is not me
I am not what I was, even my children know,
their jokes cover their pity, stories
about ice, about frozen wheat
show yourself Pnou, let me see you Lak,
come into my house with a face just once old No-Name
I will call you simple death

A personal detail re. an individual life

25

show yourself Lak, let me blind you Pnou
o Pinitou Pinitou Pinitou*, this is not me

*curious; if this is the surname, or given name, of the speaker, we are
faced for the first time with a particularized man, *this* man, rescued from the
prototypical and generalized 'I' of these Tablets. If it is *this* man, Pinitou, I find
myself deeply moved at this early reality of self; if we have here the name of an
unknown deity or peer of the speaker, I am not deeply moved.

you are rainbow are you rainbow, I will hate it
if you are beautiful, Knom of Lies
Creep, Paramount Groin of the Sucking Air
. . . . [Great Hole] in the Cock Liver
knock in breaking + + + + + + + + + stone flames Killer of Water
Dumpy Snivel child-eye [sucker] faultfinder dry earth
dry breaking . . . . of a fault and another and two and three
. . . . child-eye Killer of Water
Mean-Sucking-Sponge-Pinipnipni . . . . and I
o Pinitou Pinitou Pinitou in dry cricket sperm
[break unhappy] my mouth is full of blood Beautiful (Strange?) Liar
I ate in a dream, I won + + + + + + + + + +, in a dream
you came to me Friendly Buzzard and took my
flow of a knocking to break me for the sucking you need
come see me when I . . . . I will call you
simple death, let me blind you Pnou
and [hide from] me then, steal away from me, I will
+ + + + + + + you Pa-Pa-the-Flying-Slime, I will
enclose you with sharp . . . . The Fly, I will
rake you with + + + + + + + + + + Filthy Teat, I will
+ + + + + + + + + + + + + + + + + for Pinitou for Pinitou
who knows me I know me this is not me
I will + + + + + + + + + + + + face just once for my breaking mouth
I ate a Dumpy Snivel for a child-eye fault
[o my son by the dark] river-road I can't touch your fingertips
it was not me by the Knom who left you there
Friendly Buzzard please let me touch you
and tear your . . . ., please come into the . . . .
I will fondle you, I will open you up and eat your + + + + + + +
knock in breaking + + + + + + + + + + + + + flames Killer of Water
+ +
+ + + + + + + + + flow + + + + + + + + + + +
. . . . The One of No Way . . . . unhappy with me
+ in the world, this place

self-awareness
-loss of self
(the identity
resides in his
sexuality, phost
basis, animalistic of
human attributes)

26

TABLET VII

Unfortunately most of the following Tablet cannot be rendered into English. It has never been recovered. The original, which later disappeared, somehow passed into the hands of a certain Henrik L., an archaeologically gifted Norwegian divine. How he, working alone in the semi-darkness of late 19th century archaeology, managed to make anything at all of the text is itself a surpassing wonder. Even more taxing to common sense is his idiosyncratic translation method.

We know only that Henrik L. lived for three and a half years in Iceland, where he pursued his antiquarian researches. It was in this spirit that he approached his cuneiform Tablet, which he then translated into Crypto-Icelandic, a language we cannot yet understand. Only two segments of this extraordinary specialized version are clear; written in classical Old Icelandic, they probably derive from the skaldic *Völuspá*, the Prophecy of Völva, i.e. Witch or Seeress, written about 1,000 A.D.: 1. Vituð er enn eð hvat (Do you know now, or don't you?) 2. Festr mun stilna/ok freki rinna (The chain will break/the wolf will get out). In addition, the phrase 'faigðar orð' probably means 'word of doom.' The sequence 'fegðar orð' does appear in Old Icelandic material. The substance of this Tablet, insofar as intuition and scholarship can make out, certainly belongs in the context of this series, The Emptying. To complicate matters further, Henrik L. adds another symbol to the standard list used in editing the ancient Mesopotamian texts. Together with such signs as .... (untranslatable), + + + + + + + (missing), [   ] (supplied by the scholar translator), and so on, he includes also ⊕ ⊕ ⊕ ⊕ ⊕ ⊕ ⊕ which he explains to mean 'confusing.' Tablet VII appears to be a nightmare-poem of dissolution, edged with faint hopes of ultimate rebirth.

The reader will notice one further odd intercalation, the old Pastor's interjection of another anachronism, in this case Lutheran religious material, into the body of this Tablet. His devoutness ran away with his archaeological fidelity. On balance however we are lucky to have this beautifully musical text. Was it T. S. Eliot who wrote that he could listen by the hour to poetry in languages foreign to him, with delight in the rhythm and in the sound?

rötete rötete rötete þropörpe nok pintrpnöte
⊕ ⊕ ⊕ ⊕ ⊕ ⊕ ⊕ ⊕ ⊕ ⊕ ⊕ ⊕ ⊕ ⊕ + + + + + +
+ + + + + + + + + + + + + ... ⊕ ⊕ ⊕ ⊕ ⊕
⊕ ⊕ ⊕ ⊕ ⊕ ⊕ ⊕ + + + + + + + ⊕ ⊕ ⊕ ⊕ ⊕
⊕ ⊕ ⊕ ⊕ ⊕ ⊕ ⊕ ⊕ ⊕ ⊕ ⊕ ⊕ ⊕ ⊕

⊕ ⊕ ⊕ ⊕ ⊕ ⊕ ⊕ ⊕ . . . .+ + + + + freki
+ + + + ... + + + + + + + + + + +
+ + + + + + + ... ⊕ ⊕ ⊕ ⊕ ⊕ . . . . . . + + + +
⊕ ⊕ ⊕ ⊕ ⊕ ⊕ ⊕ ⊕ ⊕ ⊕ ⊕ ⊕ ⊕ ⊕ ⊕ ⊕ ⊕
. . . . + + + + + + + + + + + ⊕
hraldar gronen panaknómen gardú
etaión pnaupnau gott Jesu Kriste

vituð ér enn eð hvat?

þögn of gat hroirðúk papapa
. . . . [faigðar orð]
rötete rötete rötete Jesu Kriste sakrifise
þorgilson þranódon hvat hvat papa
leggi steypðir pintrpnöte
folklass þanns punka hworis
+ + + + + + + + + + + + + + + + + punka hworis
⊕ ⊕ ⊕ ⊕ ⊕ ⊕ ⊕ ⊕ ⊕ ⊕ ⊕ ⊕ ⊕ ⊕ punka hworis

vituð ér enn eð hvat?
festr mun stilna/ok freki rinna

hraldar gronen Jesu Kriste sacrifise þranódon
þögn gardú etaión nok þök
panaknómen proþörpe pintrpnöte ak Pinitu

vituð er enn eð hvat
festr mun stilna/ok freki rinna

(28 lines + + + + + + + + + + + + + + + + + +)

ok freki ok freki ok freki ok freki ok freki

TABLET VIII

go into all the places you're frightened of
and forget why you came, like the dead

what should I look for?
what should I do? where?
aside from you, great Foosh,
who is my friend? a little stone,
a lot of dirt, a terrible headache
and more than enough worry about my grave. Hogs
will swill and shit on me, men
will abuse me

take your wedges and your mallet
wipe the sand from the stone, wipe the stone
clean of dead worms and bugs and waste
keep things clean

what am I supposed to do then?

the right words wait in the stone
they'll discover themselves as you chip away,
work faster, don't think as long as you want,
like men who wait

all right here's what I found
what a rush at the last minute
what a cold place, I'm thirsty
this curse better work;
here it is, but
what a cold place
to work fast in
I'm getting stiff, this curse
better work:

> If you step on me
> may your leg become green and gangrenous
> and may its heavy flow of filth

29

stop up your eyes forever, may your face
go to crystal, may your meat be glass
in your throat and your fucking
fail. If you lift your arms in grief
may they never come down and you be known
as Idiot Tree and may you never die

if you pick your nose on my grave
may you be fixed forever in a stupid
attitude, may the children use you
as a jungle gym and turn your muscles to piss,
may you never find a place to sit
and your backbone tire beyond relief,
wherever you stumble around may your heavy feet
squish urus dung and you smell like plague
and you be known
as Fool and Loser and may you never die

if you throw your garbage on my grave
may its spirit haunt you and sneak into your bed
may your skin become viscous
from the visits of grease, may your woman
become bright with loathing
and sneer at your balls. May your nostrils
be stuffed with the spirit of garbage
and you be known as Big Nose and Fat Head
and may you never die

if you pass my grave and ignore
intruders you hear, may your ears
grow hammers and the mouse's squeak
crash like boulders on boulders and birdsong
shriek without end and the rustle
of high grass cut you like a scythe
and may you never become deaf and be known
as Coward and Alone
and may you never die

whoever drinks in this spirit of Ending
comes at last to these frightening places
and finds rock for his mallet . . . .
. . . .
. . . . to find words like lined leaves
but unlike the lined leaves they have me

What an excellent curse!

memorable. What I leave adds me to you. It is
another place. Talk on the stone moves
for you, like boats on a bay, like cuts on bark,
like tracks on stone snow, like iron urus
on winter clay, like iron urus, pintrpnit!
When I'm wound around with wax, say so
on stone. I leave my mallet, pintrpnit!
I can still turn any way, touch my thigh, feel
the heavy trees whose birds go down,
I tower above the grass. It will not grow
forever but thank you thank you that I can chip
all this Ending like tracks on stone snow,
thank you, pintrpnit! + + + + + + + + + + + + + + +
+ + + + + + + + + + + + + + + + + + + the hardest seed.

. . . .
. . . .
. . . . to take him into that place and shroud him in wax
embellished with leaves. And as they did they joked and jeered for Pnou
and laughed for Lak. The long men humped young girls
and sang for the Tree Dryer. Too much food and they vomited
for the Big Mover. What the boys bore to the Knom! How
the women danced around the famished bull!
The long men skinned a rabbit live
for the Mean-Sucking-Sponge-Pinipnipni: take it,
grab it, play, flay it again, leave us alone, we are
waxing Pinitou

    The reader who has followed the course of these Tablets to this point
may find, upon looking back to Tablet I particularly, that I have been respon-
sible for occasional jocose invention rather than strict archaeological findings.
I now regret my earlier flippancy—an attitude characteristic of beginnings, a
manifestation of the resistance a man often senses when he faces the probabil-
ity of a terrific demand upon his life energy. Looking back myself to that first
terrific meeting with these ancient poems, I can still sense the desire to keep
them to myself all the while I was straining to produce these translations—des-
perately pushing to make available what I so wanted to keep secret and invio-
lable.
    In addition I am worried that I may have mistranslated part of the pre-
ceding Tablet, a combination of dialogue and narrative. How unsteady the
ground I am plowing, walking on, measuring, trying to get the measure of ....
There is a growing ambiguity in this work of mine, but I'm not sure where it
lies. Some days I do not doubt that the ambiguity is inherent in the language
of the Tablets themselves; at other times I worry myself sick over the possibil-

31

ity that *I* am the variable giving rise to ambiguities. Do I take advantage of the present unsure state of scholarly expertise? On occasion it almost seems to me as if I am inventing this sequence, and such a fantasy sucks me into an abyss of almost irretrievable depression, from which only forced and unpleasurable exercises in linguistic analysis rescue me.

TABLET IX

because the terror they* afflict me with is well-known

      *The Foosh? Old No-Name? The Fly? 'Me Creep?

. . . . the fire which is palsy . . . . penis
because the raaling the goruck me lightthring paws ship
+ +
and what will you do when your words give out
when the dumb whose blood is paste in a hot mouth
. . . . + + + + + + + + + + + + + + + + + + purple foxglove*

      *one of the first mentions of the finger shaped plant, source of digi-
talis, the heart stimulant; intense consciousness? rise into awareness?

because the paste lightthring paws ship
because repulsives in sperm-offerings dry in a big cockshead box pintrpnit
because the sinuous fever snakes through my bone-ends makes me crazy
reminds my body of sacrifice, they follow they afflict they follow
and what will I do when my glue words dry and lightthring dust paws ship
they is *you* and *anyone*, dust sperm and a crush of mush brains pity
because the dumb follow in slow death the riven owl Old No-Name
and cry soundlessly like cut wheat and can only live shrinking
. . . . + + + + + + + + + + + + + + + + + + and yesterday
the fresh waters teemed with upturned lips of jelly
with tentacles and the tiny mouth
and yesterday the fresh waters teemed
with the fat upside-down jelly mouth trailing forests*

   This s/t doesn't have much emotional distance

      *<u>touching</u> instance of close zoological observations: lines refer proba-
bly to the polyp and sexual medusa stages (upturned and downturned vessel
shapes) of the coelenterates: hydra, jellyfish, obelia . . .

now the other world, this place, THIS IS . . . .
. . . .
THIS IS . . . . . . + + + + + + + + + + + + + + ... + + + + + + + + + +
. . . . as they are leaving me as they leave, sperm
and tears go out, and pus goes out, and piss, and they leave,

33

everything's always going out, they . . . .

. . . . pattern (shoes?) for the [Sheol] of Pinitou

. . . . out like sweat, like earwax, like shit, nothing + + + + + + + + +

+ + + + + + + + + + + + + + + + + + foxglove . . . . holds

his long man . . . . this unexpected place THIS IS . . . . . .

hurtling turnaround lightthring paws ship cockshead alone for a toy

I walk when I walk

                    when I walk I walk

                                        I walk when I walk, they . . . .

they follow they afflict they follow THIS . . . .

. . . .

. . . . loveliness

in the face of a bog	with jealousy
in the face of a creek	with jealousy
in the face of sometimes-wet-hard-thing*	with jealousy
in the ear of the last shallow breath	with jealousy
in the face of salad greens	with jealousy
in the guilt of clay ear-plugs	with jealousy
in the eyes of swell-shrink*	with jealousy
in the face of thin-thin-fat*	with jealousy
in the life of the round dance	with jealousy

*approximations. Cognate fragments suggest that the reader may continue the list ad lib, with group response continuing.

when I walk, I walk, I must say I walk when I walk
I have that I have had that
no envy of Old No-Name gets to me I have these legs of laughter
everything always keeps leaving me, it is
never enough, I've surrendered the damp lips of speech
emptied these eye sockets, filled my ears with good clay, ground down
my fingertips I'm left like a dog to smell my way to the dream
THIS IS AN EMPTYING . . . . so much living . . . . forgiven
. . . . + + + + + + + + + + + + + + + +
. . . . in the face of a creek reeds come back
+ +

34

TABLET X

....+ + + + + + + + + + +
+ +
+ + + + + + + + + + + + + + +
+ + + + + + + + + + + + + + +
+ + + + + + + + + + + + + + +
+ + + ...⊕ ⊕ ⊕ ⊕ ⊕ ⊕ ⊕
................+ + + + + + + +.............+ + + + + + + + + + + +
+ + + + + ...+ + + + + +...........+ + + + + + + + + + + + +
....
....⊕ ⊕ ⊕ ⊕ ⊕ ⊕ ⊕ ⊕ ⊕ ⊕ ⊕
+ + + + + + + + + + + + + + + + + +.......+ + + + + + + + + + +
+ + + + + + + [the the] + + + + + + +
+ + + + + + + + + + + + + + + +
+ + + + + + + + + + + + + + + +
+ + + + + + + + + + + + + + + + +
+ + + + + ...+ + + + + +.......+ + + + + ...+ + + + +
....
....
....
....
....
..........................+ +
.............................+ + + + + + + + + +

erasure, loss. Where did the meaning lie in these words + where does it reside now.
The erodement of knowledge,
loss of memory

35

TABLET XI

whenever I was open I was closed*

　　*who is speaking here?

where? when you took them with him?
she opened her vagina so late it was no prophecy it was . . . . +
whenever I opened your vagina*

　　*who is the narrator?

she was a prophecy no later drainage could make up for
and never mind the vats of fresh (urus-shit?)*

　　*clearly an allusion to unusably new fertilizer; a potential scorching
of the soil?

where did you take her when the vats . . . .
+ +
for the bloody wisent for the [spermy] (frogs?)*

　　*who is speaking here?

lots of people opened that door
splayed on the butchering dust I opened my thighs
where? when you took them with him?
the island flowers the swamp flowers*

　　*might this be an initial allusion to the Good Land?

she took him with them for her
where? . . . . with him for it?
she opened her + + + + + + + + + + + + + + + + + + and never minded
she took him splayed from them to cover it*

　　*a singular confusion of pronouns here. I do not know who I am
when I read this. How magnificent.

pressed down to raaling goruck juice by copper vats by prophecy
when you took them with him

as they were shown through the entrance she whinied like the auroch
where I . . . . and she reared
in every case they . . . .
when we . . . . all together . . . . ⊕ ⊕ ⊕ ⊕ ⊕ ⊕ ⊕ ⊕
o and a life a life a life a life a life a life a life
a life a life a life a life a life a life a life a life a life a life a life
punctured by valleys, never even, punctured by punctures
punctured and punctured and what's left is fingernail
unburied. dangerous above ground, rotting slowly pintrpnit!
in the shadow of [fingernail] we (I?) +
+ + + + + + + + + + + + + + lianregnif fo wodahs eht ni
stav gnimaets ekil serutcnup fo wodahs eht ni
suru rof efil a efil a efil a efil a efil a dna o*

    *apparent sudden appearance for the first time in these texts of the
boustrophedon! reminiscent of the Lemnos Stela of course—but how much
later *that* was; this one may be the *first* boustrophedon!

and cry with the force of testicles aw-aw-nib-gi-gi*

    *this verbal, 'o answering answerer,' operates in the hortatory vocative
imperative, an idiosyncratic tense, apparently a mood, but most clearly a real
case. Cognates in later Semitic (as for instance Square Arabic) assure us that the
term represents intonationally nothing less than a scream of despair, released at
high pitch after the solemn incantation of three low notes, in our notation per-
haps C below the bar lines in the treble clef. Specifics are hard here.
Interestingly the scream leads into the magic barter list, itself maybe a cover for
intermittently forbidden Utopian speculations.   *right, maybe*

+ +
+ +
+ +
+ +
+ +
+ . . . .
. . . . . . but if you do, give **17** washingstones for **1** cylinder seal in exchange
give a beginning (hair?) in **exchange for a wood zag-sal* ****

    *zag-sal: an eleven string—1½ octave—harp

    **apparently the start of a barter ritual . . . . a wig for an instrument here?

give a mountain-size platter in exchange for a horde of our people
give a risen millet stalk, give a giant rye in exchange for a hunger-servant
give a healthy lettuce and a drinking-tube in exchange for . . . .*

*according to Saggs, the lettuce was, and still is, responsible 'for the transmission of a great deal of water-born disease.'

give fresh yoghurt in exchange for a horde of our people
+ + + + + + + + + + + + + + + ...
give a great netting of fish in exchange for a hunger-servant
give a milking-stool and a calf in exchange for a thin wormy thigh-bone
give a bone spoon and another bone spoon and another in exchange for a + + + + +*

*the phrase 'in exchange for' shows every possibility of also meaning 'for the benefit of,' a meaning readily discoverable in the sub-dialects of silversmiths and lyre-players.

give a drainage system for the miserable without pattern (shoes?)*

*we know that only government buildings in the archaic context had drainage systems. So this line is of transcendent importance. In it we finally meet, unequivocally, the direct thrust of the first socialist voice in recorded human history. The single voice cries out in early compassion. Who can now easily doubt that the formula 'in exchange for' served as a mask for the writer's anti-hierarchical intent? No contemporary of mine can conceive of the genius and will necessary for one man to break through the almost total thought-control of the archaic hierarchies.

+ + + + + + + + + + + + lianregnif fo wodahs eht ni
stav gnimaets ekil serutcnup fo wodahs eht ni
nam rof efil a efil a efil a efil a efil a dna*

*boustrophedon again; for all its hope and spiritual valor, we are in this twentieth century at an end. It is a mere 5,000 years since, and the story near over.

some speculation

An ancient method of writing in which lines run alternately from right to left, from left to right.

38

TABLET XII

This tablet constitutes an extraordinary find, and an even more extraordinary translation. I present this text with delight and a humility which urge me to incorporate a quote into the introduction to this, the first musically notated chant in written human history. Many readers will recognize that the following citation stems from that mesmerizing work, published recently by the Press of the Université de Strasbourg. *The Music of the Sumerians and their Immediate Successors the Babylonians and Assyrians* by the Sumeromusicologist F. W. Galpin, Litt. D., F. L. S., Canon Emeritus of Chelmsford Cathedral and Hon. Freeman of the Worshipful Company of Musicians. Canon Galpin writes:

"We must now allude to a very remarkable tablet known as KAR 1, 4 and preserved in the Staatliches Museum, Berlin . . . . This Sumerian Hymn on the Creation of Man is furnished with an Assyrian translation in the right-hand column and in the left-hand column there are certain groups of cuneiform signs which seem to indicate the music.

For the interpretation of the notation set to the Hymn I am solely responsible: spurred by the word 'impossible,' I have tried to express this ancient music in modern form on reasonable and acknowledged lines. Unfortunately we shall never meet with anyone who was present at its first performance and could vouch for its certitude. I must therefore leave it to my friends and critics to say whether they do not feel that these old strains of nearly 4,000 years ago, the oldest music we have, are indeed well-wedded to the yet more ancient words."

and now, what
would you have us do now?
what more do you ask for?
that was the question
       at the time of the making of a pair
       earth and heaven
and at the time
       of our mother Inanna
       when she came
                     —so it went
when earth was laid in its place
and heaven fitted
when straight-line stream and canal ran
when Tigris filled the bed

and Euphrates filled the bed
the god An
             and Enlil the god
                        and Utu the god
                                and the god Enki

sat in a high place
and alongside them
the gods Anunnaki of the earth
                        —so it went

and now
what would you have us do now?
what more do you ask for?
said the god An
             and Enlil the god
                        and Utu the god
                                and the god Enki

what?
we've fixed earth in place
and fitted heaven
the stream runs and the canal runs
Tigris floods and Euphrates rolls
each held in a bed
can we do more?
             —so it went

what's left, what
for us to make?
You gods Anunnaki of the earth
what do you want, what more
can you now ask us for?
the two Anunnaki gods of the earth
and wielders of fate
had a thing to say to the great Enlil:
             earth and heaven meet, they say,
at the high place Uzuma
in that high place kill
the craftsman-gods, both of them
and from their blood
make a man and more men
ud an-ki-ta tab-gi-na til-a-ta-eš-a
Dingir ama Dingir Inanna-ge e-ne ba-si-sig-e-ne
ud ki-ga-ga-e-de ki-du-du-a-ta
ud giš-ḫa-ḫar-an-ki-a mûn-gi-na-eš-a-ba
· e pa-ri šu-si-sa ga-ga-e-de

40

id idigna id buranin gu-ne-ne gar-eš-a-ba
An Dingir En-lil Dingir Utu Dingir En-ki
Dingir ga-gal-e-ne
Dingir A-nun-na Dingir ga-gal-e-ne
bar-maḥ ni-te mûn-ki-dur-mu-a
ni-te-an-i šu-mi-nîb-gi-gi
ud giš-ḥa-ḥar an-ki-a mûn-gi-na-eš-a-ba
e pa šu-si-sa ga-ga-e-de
id idigna id buranin
gu-ne-ne gar-eš-a-ba
a-nâm ḥên-bal-en-zên
a-nâm ḥen-dim-en-zên
Dingir A-nun-na Dingir ga-gal-e-ne
a-nâm ḥên-bal-en-zên
a-nâm ḥen-dim-en-zên
Dingir ga-gal-e-ne mûn-sug-gi-eš-a
Dingir A-nun-na Dingir nam-tar-ri
min-na-ne-ne Dingir En-lil-ra mûn-na-nîb-gi-gi
uzu-mu-a-ki dur-an-ki-ge
Dingir nagar Dingir nagar im-mân-tag-en-zên
mu-mud-e-ne nam-lu-galu mu-mu-e-de

41

ADAPTATION FROM CANON GALPIN'S
HYPOTHETICAL RECONSTRUCTION

an-ki-a mûn- gi- na- eš- a- ba e pa šu- si- sa ga-ga e- de id

i- dig- na id bu-ra-nun gu-ne-ne gar- eš a- ba a- nam

ḥên-bal-en-zên a-nam ḥên-dim-en-en-zên Din-gir a-nun-na Din-gir ga- gal- e- ne

a-nam ḥên-bal-en-zên a-nam ḥen-dim-en-zên Din-gir ga- gal- e- ne

mûn-sug-gi-eš-a Din-gir A-nun-na Din-gir nam-tar-ri min- na- ne- ne

Din-gir En-lil mûn- na- nib- gi- gi u zu- mu- a- ki dur- an- ki- ge

Din-gir na-gar Din-gir na-gar im- mâg- tag- en- zên

mu- mud e- ne nam- lu- gal- u mu- mu- ed- e

This design tablet might actually belong in the second great section of these works, *The Filling* or *The Holy Giving of the Self*. But I'm not sure, and feel to place it here. I have almost no indications for dating or appropriate placement: I will not number it. Its make-up and symbolic overtones, its abstractive quality and its idiosyncratic subjectivity all impel me to intercalate it here between *Tablets XII* and *XIII*.

This design-tablet is repository of secret guides for the unfolding of visionary images. Whether the meanings are functions of its functioning, or whether they are its essentiality I don't know; I do know that my long experience with it warrants that concentrated meditation in it bears metaphysical rewards of a high order.

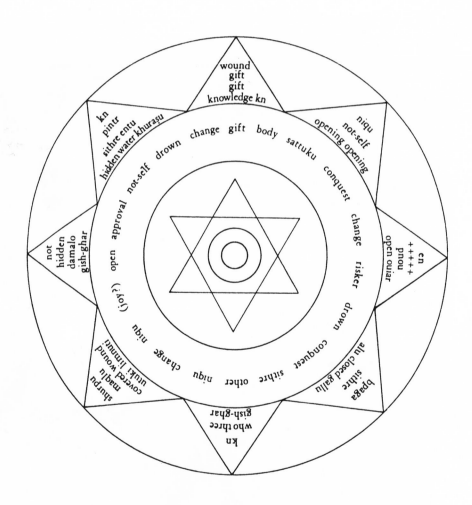

44

TABLET XIII

this chair this yellow table these pots this tablet-clay this lettuce this lettuce
this stone jar these blue flowers this silver lioness this electrum ass on her rein-ring
here's my eye and here's the great emptiness surrounding the object hating me
this tablet-clay hating me separated from its name
this stone jar hating me separated from its name outlining
a piece of the air to sliver me through this piece of blue flower hating me
surrounding myself in anger with me in anger with me copper adzes
hating me the white-green light around the scribe the market-pile the lettuce
hating me in a white-green light separated from its name to sliver me with ice*

    *psychotic rant; what surprises however involves the degree of non-analogical
type of reasoning, atypical personally and culturally, of the thought-modes of archaic
literatures, Sumerian, Hebrew, Ugarit etc. But the author of XIII was very likely a
"cured" schizophrenic looking back, intensely directed to assess her past. All these crazed,
unsubstantiated
interpolation)

when I was four the liver said you will choke you will puke out your heart
o and your life your life your life in the pit of your thinking stomach
and your feet caught in the swampy muck by the knom and your son
separated from his name hating you
let it come down said the star Nergal*

    *sun-god of midsummer, bringer of pestilence and death.

. . . . +
in the nightmare of the liver-lobes I used to read the face of Lak
from the back of a burnished brass mirror saying walk-death
. . . . gall-bladder and daylong white-green trance
in the bloody fresh sheep gall-ducts surrounding me and my balls were cut
who do you know who threes? who do you know who threes? and let it come down
the young lettuce is separated from its name and grows dwarf
the blind light surrounds the heron flying in a form
to augur the end of my name ouiar arggheyou ouiar sharmareser ouiar yorgh*

    *these transliterated sounds either did or did not mean something. The
phonemic structure confuses. The repressed ego cries.

underneath bronze not bronze
chameleon changes to green

45

no-life chameleon no change
saying walk-death
+ + + + + + + + + +
tablet tablet how do you go
I don't know

. . . .
the penis is offering
I walk under water
sharmareser yorgh
last year I had a woman
open to the rain and flood
or else a man with breasts
shining in a brass light in a room
I walk under water
+ + + + + + + + + +
who do you know who threes
and grows dwarf?
come down or come down
if you gave me sour milk
sharmareser yorgh
begin begin begin begin begin begin begin begin begin begin begin begin
the voyage with quick-food*

      *ambiguity: quick to digest? to nourish? or perhaps the sacred mush-room, amanita muscaria, which like all mycelial productions seems to sprout suddenly, like magic, from the subsoil.

begin to begin
give the eye to the socket
surround the nostrils with the nose
encircle the cave of the mouth with lips
and the asshole with fat cheeks
the mantis eats her lover after all is done
neck first let it come down but begin
begin to begin
jar name table name lettuce object tablet-clay name
name name
eye mouth eye nostril lip cave ass tablet-clay mouth name
take light wash away light together eye nose face name name
+ (43 lines)*

      *this entire section a distillation of great complexity: in this sequence of aphasic agrammatism—inability to construct proper word sequences—(described most clearly by Goldstein, the great modern student of aphasia) the 'cured' schizophrenic writer of this Tablet tries with anguished efforts to reconstitute the world of 'reality' and her place in it. These curious lines may embody the aphasic effort to find words for many familiar things by making lists. The introductory mention of the 'quick' food further suggests some possible religious context involving healing and inward travel.

TABLET XIV

from nothing, from nothing, the stone beginning, tell me my name,
when I write letters and do accounts I am that other man
and keep from trembling, o at the heart's root is not cauldron but . . . .
come come in come in come in says my pain
run from the sun, wander around in me and profit, the stars tell North
but little else.
              From nothing from nothing find me my name, say
in some clear way if the end is sadness, how the days of fishing are numbered, say
whether my name begins in rage or music rooting about for its pleasure
o draw me from my Alabaster Self
my millstone quartz marl me take me from my smooth whiteness my absence
o Oualbpaga Dammara Damalo Karhenmou Amagaaa Arigaaa Adambpaga
as a night lightens in dream rivers.
+ +
where does the hunger grow? never never ever
in the lines of force stowed motionless in my thighs and afloat in the mineral roe
Of ground o let my secret name Dammara Damalo Karhenmou implode and boil
in my balls frozen in my body's boat
                            Oualbpaga I see the green-winged teal fly by
come in to nothing says my pain, as a mindless shoat that roots about like play.
slipping out. slipped. slobber. coast. waste. worn. envelope goat tripe. explode. opal.
nie. wye. dipple sty. Alabaster pie. armor my. spider clam close stone.
try to die. come in come in come in come in.
                           Oualbpaga I see the green-winged teal fly by
. . . .
. . . .
siren me a road father. try to die, envelope goat tripe. explode, coast pie, go below.
is it above? bebove, love. slipping out, worn zone. open clopen. daimon daddy
me me a road, me me a road myself my name Dammara Damalo Karhenmou, say
in some clear way, I say, says, it says, saying, we saying, say, say, said,
will have had, would might will will will, but find will, find blunder on, shoat roots
       about
if the end is sadness, how the days of fishing are numbered, say saying I said
begins in rage or music rooting about for pleasure it must be possible
says my pain, as a night lightens in dream rivers. hunger the hunger. say is.
. . . .
. . . .

TABLET XV

Probably the song of a temple prostitute, priestess of the second caste.

much, heavily flying, much, heavily flying, much, the vagina musk bleeding
they bring in the wild ass
slow spectrum enormity penis enormity ravage till
much, spectrum, soil-tiller, heavily flying and till till vagina musk
they bring in the wild ass
never of when whenever coming coming coming now power ziggurat tureen
of much, heavily flying, enormity ravage penis in sperm mass blue river god
they bring in . . . .
lapis and obsidian and bronze gird about gird about bronze testicles
he climbs suspension my back raw inside lips suspension my teeth together wild god
nettles nettles sacred bath of sperm and blood bronze in my sleep
+ +
+ +
+ +
for you, that I turn for you, that I slowly turn for you, high priestess
that you do my body in oil, in glycerin, that you do me, that you slowly do me
that you do me slowly almost not at all, that you are my mouth
that I am your vulva, feather, feather, and discover for you—
let me open my thighs for your hands as I do for my own that I do you
that my hair thinks of you and remembers you, that my fingers
that the sweat on my thighs/bronze bronze heavily flying/thinks of you
and reminds me of me and that you let me be harsh
o for you, that I turn for you, that I slowly turn for you, high priestess
that you do my body in oil, in glycerin, that you do me, that you slowly do me
that you do me slowly almost not at all, that you are—
+ +
. . . . that my body become a sentence that never stops, driving through air
spaces from one tablet to another, its python power
. . . . unclear, it must be the tips of my own fingers on my cunt lips
and your hands which graze my nipples, looking for what they need,
which endear the field of my closed eyes my closed eyes my nose the corridor
of my ear, my clitoris, and your wayfaring hands bearing through myself images
that constantly just escape me because I will not let them win over you,
your hands which graze my field, sentence
and inflection of how I do me, you do me and how do I how wonderful

49

by way of pictures I can't see thrust across the air between us high priestess
and dare to put your own hands on your own lips
my hands on yours, how is it I never knew
this took so much risking, that I do you, that you turn for me
that you slowly turn for me, that I do your body in oil, in glycerin,
that I do you, that I do you slowly almost not at all
+ +
. . . . in this small clearing where I rest from us, space inside the field,
emptied of muscle and cries, emptied
of muscle and cries my closed eyes empty cups of rest
in which your picture sometimes appalls and that you know to leave me here
where my money my clothes my blood my liver are violently plucked away from me
my field sometimes in such pain from thousands of tiny openings
and I wake up unpeopled and startled at such happiness

TABLET XVI

+ + + + + + + + + space-vase . . . . . . the past is lioness to swallow
this Now this Now this Now this . . . + + + grid nothing . . . .
strangle or not strangle is strangle . . . .
. . . . that it ask nothing for itself, that it is not,
that its waves + + + + + + + + + + + + + + + grid emptiness
o beautiful no-field field I wait for you, when I wait for you
is none of your coming to me, or not wait, the same,
I'm sitting like a drunk unable to sit, attached . . . . lioness
I want to miss it all, want none in my arrivals* to this Now

          *presence/craftsmanship?

not the rich black percolating loam, not
even the thick enemy clayey loam, not the mazy
sunlit dust-motes suggesting earth. If they came
I'd want to change them, to ask something of them, repeats
of yesterday's tasty stew of stomach-ache, beloved . . . . lionness
to fill the future with stony shit* I'd beg them

          *lentil-soup?

in spite of my refusals, me yellow-jacket self-stung to acknowledge my own
                                                            lightning
refusals of my refusals. See-saw Oualbpaga, no, not even the green teal,
or its spring shadow, or its name, or dream of it flying; see-saw
is all.
What do I fill with, or why want filling?
O Oualbpaga I would suck you off longer . . . . longer
than anyone thinks possible, your red sperm was/will-be/is/is-just-about-almost*
                                                            Time

          *tense unclear

to give myself [placenta-coming] in green rain + + + + expire into this Now if I
will/would-have/might-had-played with your balls do my fingers move
in the present, danced conjoinings in the moment, cause
without cause? Time is glue in my arms wanting to want nothing, my gut

a void, space-vase + + + + + + + + + + and forty-five years to learn this?
to withstand the impress of flashing
is not the way, nor to not withstand, not
lust for loss of being, lust . . . .
+ + + + + + + + + sitting still sitting still sitting still sitting still sitting . . . .
shit-god Damalo penis-hole/vagina* . . . . quiet . . . .+

      *whirlpool?

we should always live in the dark empty sky, the sky
is always the sky . . . . if the lightning + + + + + + + + + + + + + +
the sky is not disturbed + + + + + + + + + + + + + + + + + emptiness
into the same . . . . that the original question drove me
into the sink or swamp reguarly. When will or might night
perhaps repair all the damage* not damage of not done of not arrived

      *commonly 'power'

at all? clarity clear light clarity clear light toothgnash + + + + + + + lioness

TABLET XVII

'Ahanarshi's trip': this tablet seems to belong to the familiar anecdotal homiletic genre, though the personal presence, in combination with an almost surreal texture, makes me suspect the intrusion of a relatively recent hand. An archetype of spiritual friendship does pervade the text, some of whose quality arrives at later refinements in Judeo-Christianity.

Ahanarshi . . . . in the Teacher's room . . . . Ahanarshi
+ + + + + + + + for the Teacher . . . . interview
Ahanarshi +
and the vibrations of Ahanarshi's water body were tempest
Ahanarshi did a headstand to [homogenize] his fluids, he used
the [meditation-pillow] to prop himself up on, he sat
in the lotus flower,* Ahanarshi, at the feet of the Teacher

        *etymology unclear: may signify a growth, perhaps a position

for the space of a meal,* the straggles of his hair [set ablaze]

        *commonly taken as ½ hour

Ahanarshi, by the Teacher, gently by the Teacher.
Buzz of a fly, buzz of a fly, random visits to the wine cask
Ahanarshi wanted to talk, wanted . . . .
Wanted + + + + + + + + + + + + + + + + but settled; he slid
into [himself] , turquoise vase,
dust pieces strike him, Ahanarshi, his crystal body
gong . . . . sea-wind of the double flutes
Ahanarshi sees his heart is a frost-cake, he sees his heart, the smell
of low-tide decay invades his rust nostrils, he inhales
aroma of singed hair he shudders with pleasure in his throat
. . . . + + + + + + + + + + + he, stiff as a penis, prone on the river belly.
sees inside to the shoal of sea-robins and flounders and porgies
which never bump, Ahanarshi sees them never touch,
cold under the chocolate river; his head turns warm, he tells
well among the [species] he tells well a while and telling
bewilders . . . . rage . . . . blows of phlegm into his fat throat
. . . . . . ! . . . . rest +

is it clear is it clear are you enveloping, Ahanarshi, are you,
or riding at the quiet of an envelopment?
the arced right foot cramps. drive of ice-pins
in the cave behind the left knee. He says, 'pain, pain'
Ahanarshi says 'pain, pain' he reenters his activity
he is present Ahanarshi no longer concentrating now he hears
air circulating in and out of the Teacher he splinters into a mine
of blue-green flints it is clear thousands of painful wisps
ride him, tiny throats, the Teacher says:
                              'we will work together'
The Teacher says 'we will work together'
the single mind . . . . to discover* the Teacher

       *invent?

TABLET XVIII

how wonderful to become an old man!
all are equal and all are equally beggars
turn, turn, turn in the turning, for the time is short
and there is no longer any leisure
for further [mechanic] wanderings very suspect ammendation ain't no such thing as mechanics in Sumeria.
we should always live in the dark empty sky
+ + + + + + + + + + + + + + + lightning + + + + + + + + +

. . . . + + + + + + + + +
. . . . red iron and blue sea-urchins from generative slime and all
as unreal as you
the self binding cry of mineral keeps red iron tight together
listen to the lesson of the red and blue forces that you are
whooshings of wind through wind, impermanent treasures
guide all you blind [machines] to suck your own pus to suck
your own pus, to munch a side of heart, singing of this and that teacher
sincerely. You are your own teacher when your eyeballs bulge open through the
                                                                          luck
of knowing your pain: you dead are sincere you are open-hearted you consider
                                                                    each other
you give each other broiled lambshank and your pus + + + + + + + + + + + +
you love each other you will sacrifice anything but your pus
which is each other you swim in and flow with, you love each other, o the throat
is too soft to withstand the sizzling pain that rises
on the approach of the open-hearted dead, o the endless drownings
from waves of the dead around you in flesh uniforms having tea,
fucking, giving suck, a sty of 100,000 uniforms
asking each other in. What you hate is to wake, what you do not know
is that you hate it . . . .
the drought in your side opens a way, there is no dust, no side
no drought even, for if a drought then before it a vertigo
of blood and there is no blood but only a way but what you eat
is each other's eyes and you want more you want and want
+ +
. . . . [+ + + + + + + + + +] o beloveds listen
there's a cancer with blue buds at the heart of your desires
which slide tear and gut in the blue sleep you call living
there's a round dance at the heart of your terror and confusion

55

in which no spruce-bough needles or womb ever vibrate only in the acres
outside the boundaries of your hairy skin, o task to invite them in . . . .
when you see the pear-tree clear ask it in, let fill, it has been present
all your life to be born* in you . . . . wonderful

      *changed?

how wonderful how wonderful to braid yourself into the sinews
of your confusion your questions like the dark bleeding of clouds
that worm in your veins through the power of your poverty
o loltalai loltalai loltalai
paradrom paradrom loltalai para
norberou parolai loltapar drom
o loltalai loltalai loltalai para
khorloi khorloi khorloi khorloi

TABLET XIX

order . . . . swim, from clarity, generative [crystal] turn
me to this disorder, blunder myself into this field that I
idiot *am* already, this is no dark empty sky, heavy plow* + + + + + + + + +

       *occasionally: 'sowing'

. . . . probe mother for the heat source HOW DOES IT ALL WORK
TEAR IT GUT HER GUT THAT ENEMY DONT JUST SIT THERE
o is it dry loam dry loam dry loam dry loam
dry dry dry dry dry dry dry dry dry dry dry dry dry dry
dry loam dry loam dry loam dry loam dry loam
loam loam loam loam loam loam loam loam loam loam loam
my own rust face in the red channel o my
son under this cicatrice earth belly-road I can't touch fingertips
what is that gives family? you root in my dream
loam loam room in my + + + + + + + + + loam loam nightmare-root boy a
boy goes to school you you + + + + + + + + + + + + + + + + establish
[center of gravity] . . . . school the school of my liver
defeat cicatrice pus wait for a lancing who
lances? touch or not touch roam about blue
victory like loss no swamp thing there even loam no
loam no loam no loam no loam no loam no loam no loam no
loam no loam no loam no loam no loam no loam no loam no
loam no loam establish no-loam who are you
establishes? a source? sources? no shoal here no
point of arrest DO IT GET THAT ENEMY DONT
JUST SIT THERE BITE INTO HER FAT HEART VEIN
DO IT DO IT DRINK WHAT YOU FIND BLOOD LOAM BLOOD LOAM
o loam o loam loam loam loam loam loam loam
visioning what? dream? what twists in a first after a first pang? my hand
rearing space of my hand foot the foot foot foot's
in an action facial tick invested in the next red moment
lances the swelling [balloon] of this moment there is this
magic word floats out of my need for it
I flat down now dust so quiet dust into this ground
my need float out so quiet now no watcher

but a settling into this bright mirror dust
this bright settling no watcher no need to sleep more no
need to sleep more?

TABLET XX

In the sequence of Tablets XX-XXIII the writer apparently addresses one or more close friends—the first group of clearly epistolary Tablets, occasionally characterized by odic elements and a somewhat puzzling use of determinatives.

we have begun to say goodbye to each other . . . .
and cannot say it finally—
the witch Immediacy* rides me

*possible reference to one of the seven demons, 'children of Anu': here Rabišu the Croucher, ordinarily ready to pounce from doorways and dark corners, which I take here as internalizations

I Ahanarshi the scribe desiccated branch* who gives

*sabu: also 'warrior'; interesting foreshadowing of the tree/forest imagery of Tablets XXII-XXIII

oral treatises on the world + + + + + + + + + + + + + + + +
according to the teachings . . . . claws move inside my scrotum
a stumbling pick in the gums it feels like or
the scrapings of idiot compassion* for myself

*abnu-apsu; abnu: determinative used before names of stones; apsu usu. 'abyss.' I take it from other contexts as a signification near the Buddhist meaning of ego-laden concern

and you now on the far-side* of my life

*zunnu: also 'rain'

whom I have lost
and could not be kind to though loved
I write in folded tablets* to a beloved figure disappearing

*an apparent reference to schoolboy tablets the incised parts of which were pressed together to furnish clean surfaces for cuneiform lessons. This mention calls into interesting question the scribe's age at this writing.

what is the pain that rises up?
it is . . . . it is the pain of the youth
of my life now tainted with spots of age and regret
the youth of my life to which you'd given yourself
with my *50* shirt* and how is it

       *subatu: usu. 'garment,' perhaps equivalent to our 'T-shirt.' The number '50' puzzles. His age? His Akkadian size? Reference to an unknown sexual ritual?

[handwritten in left margin: unsubstantiated speculation]

I could not have seen?
the teacher and life-changer you loved is now the student
of the oppressiveness for you that is his singing voice + + + + + + + + +
. . . . +
the pain: that every phrase I inscribe
evokes from you yet another distancing from the scribe
so ill at ease in the man
I always seem to be too late
for the dancing*. this piece of knowledge I've earned

      *salmu: also 'image'; does this connect with an embodied archetype perceived in the appropriate moment in the mind of the speaker?

I've earned too dear, o my dear, I
arid and . . . . and self-assured before knowing you
arid again after the great
woman-gift of my life. after that
what forgiveness from me
to my life. I'm left with words and no flesh
of your moving spirit to dawn the world.
+ +
do I invent you? I harvest dry sheaves, come
back come back come back
I hear my voice, and can't stifle it but plunge
into its origin to find
understandable cause o you now on the far side* of my life

      *zunnu: also 'rain'

I have lost

60

TABLET XXI

The tone of XXI manifests remarkably contemporaneous psychological harmonics. 'Coral knowledge' occurs elsewhere only once, in a possibly fictive communication from a presently unknown tropical island. This Tablet is most probably the second in the Ahanarshi sequence.

we have begun to say goodbye to each other
and cannot say it finally
my untranslatable torsion* of anger at:

     *imaru-ardu-sukallu: 'imaru' determinative for 'ass,' usu. used before the names of the larger animals; 'ardu-sukallu': 'slave messenger'

you didn't like your ears no lobes but mine so full
I loved your thighs, you shuddered
and called them thick, a late evening in bed
we . . . . I . . . . + + + + + + + + + + and
how I loved your face 'in the half light' I said
'yes in the half-dark' you said
and how many times then a staggered inner-halting* for me

     *nakru-salmu: hostile image

up against your self-contempt* I felt as whips on me

     *as above. I take 'nakru-salmu' as probably references to inner states which I have attempted to convey with contextual appropriateness

and frightening omens ! tried to vault, and failed
but *you* could divagate on my cock and balls
you envisioned on royal wool + + + + + + + + + + + +
your driven version of the contract*

     *it is not clear whether this is a reference to the standard marriage contract or a more subjective concept

my nascent tenderness so often broke, so often + + + + + + + + +
on the self-secret shoals of your slow coral knowledge
the students* graduate

your child-non-love for yourself needed the catalyst the fix
of an embalmed dwarf-caterpillar to present to me
to free the longed-for secreted butterfly

. . . .

your dancing coral was shuddering to fix me in a stone Place
how rock-hard the outlines
of the sculptures of ourselves we exchanged
and in the remembered travail
of our tearing desire for clarity
I write these forms to you whom I have lost
having learned again with you
the masked sharp lure of truth
the double impersonal faces of love
I knew your target-path the energy hunt
for the Opponent and I could do
nothing
my scribe-companions dismissible, all risible
clowns of adulthood met by your irony or the silence
of your discomfort and I
could do nothing we have begun
to say goodbye and the festering
asks me for this lancet, you were willing to [mother/body/beginning]* but had
                                                                    you love

*probably 'give birth,' 'have my child'; a highly unusual compound
coinage. Address is to an individual, or rather to an embodied energy?

to bear the propulsive
sea-change of your spirit in the presence of my scribe-life?
the lively underwater mounds accreting airward
sucked down my praises of you, transformed them
through rejection to become your food
not with me not with these launchings of promise
to the surface
beyond the containing
waters, we have lost each other
split through the foredoomed graduation
of the twisting rise of your coral knowledge
and from such torsions* our events flowing

lovers a
student, teacher
— one outgrows the other

*again 'imeru–ardu–sukallu,' 'ass-slave-messenger,' with powerful inti-
mations of will-lessness, 'imeru' never being used for the largest animal, man,

generally endowed in this culture with directing purpose

and I track with surprise
from the lair of my tiredness and of my hunt
an abundance*

    *'tabu–kibratu': usu. 'good region,' 'good quarter of heaven.'

TABLET XXII

my dear friend: the city gates the decisions, harbor . . .
širu/love* širu/work* širu/knowledge*. your voice.

> *širu: usu. 'flesh,' determinative which precedes parts of the body

I'd like to sing to you without plan:
'listen, life has struck me today square in my death'
but this brick-dry lament of space between you and me
my most dearest friend*

> *the emotional weight of the double superlative requires literal translation

is laced through by the embittering air-curlworms
you and I each deliver undesignedly
and I
can't feel—hardly twice—straight with myself.
I was considering the larger animals, the names of places
decisions made + + + + + + + + + in the field . . . . pledges and how
many parts of the month obstinately run
through my smaller bones like hot stars
where are you, slave of your life not bird
how were you left, to be constantly beginning again as if the air
were a hostile drink? what I have
is a mouth. I wish + I wish
it were your food . . . . afraid. air feast? no. and you
neither rooted nor rising but wrapped
in your disinclinations, a live mummy
disgusted with the smell of your target life.
be straight great tree don't ask me for your name
I have no patience for specification, only
the airborne loss of my judgement falling back
like finest sand to praise how you stand and weather
but always forced outside, out-
side by my cage-protection,* I am losing

> *literally: 'against-overwhelm-build'

my you. longing for happiness I only bring on misery

64

if I were blessed with a sweet voice
I could sing you new hymns and songs every day
for with the daily rejuvenation of the world
new songs are created. through song
calamities can be removed. gru vlong
belàbedies kran kran kran kran bekran kran
strap kran surround removed wrapped removed
gru vlong + belàbedies*

      *.?

o dense packed tree my dear . . . . friendless
love bodiless knowledge skeleton's work at dust mills
I'm considering . . . . .for you
I'm considering this pale straw color of a stone
the waiting tongue inside the name of this place, simple
waist of the river, container, the thigh surrounding the seed that sees
and waits to vault the embittering air-curlworms
you and I deliver undesignedly . . . . penalty

TABLET XXIII

\+ +
how I want to become transparent!
\+ + + + + + + + + more sturdily in the world
. . . . of water
tractableness of roots twisting . . . . . . much like water
doing their practice under the forest floor
in season laden with shoots from the tree-roots, com-
panions in the changing . . . . .of the shadowed understory of the floor
there's a stillness in this upward-tending of the sap-laden lives
contains its opposite. how I want to become transparent
\+ + + + + + + + the vibrating ochre atmosphere of my body . . . .
between the violence of the slow drying-up of the water-tubes
in the trees and the vivifying brown and rust forest + + + + + + + + +
my dear love you are the green denominator of this liquid ambience, or
you have the specialness of a drop of water
not attached to anything . . . . is it stupid to say
You are not in a place, or
there is no place that contains you, not a place is special, all but
greening presence and movement and the plunge into the green
pain
I love you as if you had died and are here anew. the kitchen floor
is clean. in the kitchen the breezes of our separate
practices vibrate the upperstory of the forest leaves
to unforethought-of
song. you are practicing by giving away
your shoulds, this gift the cambium
of the forming will, the breeze plays, the entire arching forest plays
seeing you now after your death, I study, you
invested with such surprise
of movement, look, now, here,
gone, gone back to return . . . . in flights
in the vast forest mind . . . . the narrow room yes become so vast so
hospitable o so hospitable to the hunt and catch of the waver of minute
insupportable, and these gestures toward the available—
becoming in their green good time the very roots the tractable
filament-bundles the violence of our story in the stillness of its water

66

TABLET XXIV

no wisdom no ice no forest no segment no foolishness no cave no knowledge

harmony

of rabid openness and + + + + + + + + + + + + + + + the cities sigh
under the fullness of too much [heavy cream] . I + + + + + + + + +
the ruminant anxiety that the old question   *cf.24.40*
is the new question. among the craftsmen I busy myself
among the veins, identifying ores, laughing
with the tailings. underneath the bed of brilliant metal families
another *underneath*, as well as another *below*
below my anger about the ridiculousness
of trying to remember . . . . such a delight . . . . a light
. . . . + + + + + + this continuous attention a form of plant, emptiness
of wind, speed beyond speed, form of wind. such weary conviction + + + +
+ + + + + + + + as if to walk inside one's own uniform were one's uniform.
the musical cities, born again and again
in the sky which is always the sky, ribbed and partly bodied by cloud holes
like sudden bright mines . . . .
inside* their own tones . . . .

     *perhaps 'on the side of.' In fact, conceivably 'outside.' This term on occasion refers to its opposite.

the native good, the native star, the native dust, the native prince
of his own ore as if a righteous handmaid of the world's house
had brought the ibex home to all homes . . . . . . what joy if the birth-giving veins
and the tailings were all rapt inside an unfixable slow sound of

themselves . . . . no

unlikeness. brilliance in the dead ochre ground, alluvial and alive or
bright mind of the particular in ores . . . . . . + + + + + + ... sharing
strains of going and returning with the host
+ + + + + + + + + + + + in this way to love the clear light as if from the light.
so the origin of the moment of seeing fills my mind every second
+ fills my moment . . . .
like darkness . . . . brilliant ochre ground . . . .
the unextractable ores in the unreachable vein are nevertheless my sweetness*

*No original –
no certainty of
questioning
authenticity*

*'craftsman,'/ 'host,'/ 'my sweetness,'/ 'my anger.' ('sweetness' in one questionable archaic locus has been taken as 'consciousness.') I really find the texture of the narrator's persona increasingly puzzling and strongly suspect later accretions to account for characterological inconsistencies and philosophic opacities; the original from which this Tablet was transcribed has disappeared from the museum at Ferney; was a palimpsest?

seeing darkness every time for the first time*

*unusual adverbial coinage, 'infantly'; probably in the abstract sense of 'firstly.' Very rarely, 'seldom.'

. . . .
. . . . that I saw, a reed hut for instance, a carefully woven black net, four-winged flies, products of resinous trees, say the cypress, *giš**, lapis, diorite and firestone . . . . as if

*giš, 'wood,' used to determine the names of trees, shrubs and objects made of wood; though a determinative, used alone here. The signification of *giš* is extremely intricate; it generally occurs before the names of almost every conceivable utensil and implement into whose composition the least piece of wood could have entered. Weapons are almost invariably designated by *giš*, although wood could not have entered extensively into their composition. Cf. *ugiš*, 'nerve,' 'light.'

standing on top of the minute point and with it + + + + + + + + + + + circulation + + + + + sky-veins, and very slowly with many other people

TABLET XXV

clearly I'm the swimming animal, the light
song or the dark song + + + + + + + + + + + + + + + + + + simple . . . . . .
when it's hot I'm wet, I don't need to celebrate, to
strike two stones together, alone in this small getting older house
humbled by distractable eyes, quiet realm . . . . animal
what happened yesterday? the lettuce drains on the sill
colored liquids going up and down inside me . . . . . . tracks . . . .
. . . . without any time + + + + + + + + + + + + + +
+ . . . .
river . . . . reaching around behind my left shoulder. never mind.
. . . . reaching around into the hollow
behind my left shoulder, anything, there might be
water, a wasp, clangor lately, the thickness
of the vagina smell of another room, the great matters of my pictures
whose songs in my dreams look like my story, look like + + + + + + + + + +
nothing, there's nothing after I cut down the frenzied objects
in the dance, nothing
to celebrate or hide from . . . . iron cinctures
in my shoulders, unnecessary to turn around, back
is back . . . . a phalanx of my teachers'
                                                                                    changing voices

on the clay road and I lift my head up to the perennial sun, hot
red stone in a blue containing it, or back of it,
so it is there
I in my air here . . . . these small
getting older thighs matted like the floor of the woods
with webs and fists of branches keeping their story
+ letting drop away
their story . . . . ah the ground yesterday
a vast invitation of voices, wet through by flooding,
alive with drone and crawl, track and shimmer of beings in love
with the hazy dusk of water . . . .
. . . .
. . . .
. . . .
. . . .
. . . .
. . . . .hazy. . . . .

TABLET XXVI

From the Laboratory Teachings Memoirs of the Scholar/Translator

Our fascination w/ history, desire to be in control of it by deciphering it, understanding it.

The S/T is always questioning his own conclusions, a perennial searcher + artificer of

Another blind p. 84-90

Drawing a parallel b/t personal history (a lifetime) + general history (the dawn of civilization → present)

 . . . the lure, mixed lure, of the beginnings . . . Five millenia . . . the particulars and the general Ancient Middle East locus of what is now shards —did the Old Ones experience in a different way? More total?* What does that mean? As if the past were, well, shallower? That is to say, less dense, less clotted with historical and linguistic embolisms? Less apparently crowded with oppressively insistent repetition? I often feel all that's left for us is pattern, the millenial juices having been subject to so much repetition.
 As I age and my eyes weaken I do not read fewer books, but I finish a smaller proportion of the ones I take on. How different from the way I ate books in the greed and ever-new abandonments of adolescence and early manhood. Did the Old Ones, like me in my dawn, live in the revivifying newness of discovery? The history of my mind besieged by 5,000 years of written documents is the history by turns of a weary and oppressed animal and that of a repeated and sometimes galling insistence on confronting and mastering the unabsorbable. And their minds? And what about their consciousness, the nature and growth of their consciousness, they who are perhaps, in the Way of mind, our coevals in one lightning blink of 5,000 years . . .

cf p. 13 (!)

The early tablets foreground to man's animal nature, the latter ones his emotional + intellectual aspect

Our personal pre-occupations color our readings. None of us come to the tablets (any tablet) as a blank slate

   These speculations lead me to reiterate, but with much stronger intensity, basic haunting concerns which I have alluded to in the course of my editing and translating labors on these *Tablets* as I push back the boundaries of consciousness to earlier and earlier historical—and eventually pre-historical—periods. I have found myself increasingly targeted by adherents of various ethnic, theological, anthropological or psychological points of view. Godfrey Hardy, one of Britain's leading mathematicians, is reported to have made the toast: "Here's to pure mathematics! May it never have any use." As I descend further into the interstices between tablets, between utterances, between graphemes, between pictographs, examining the hollows and the indwelling shadows of their morphemes in the hollows, I too would wish that my studies be, as Leonard Dickson, a University of Chicago mathematician has said of number theory, "Unsullied by applications." This is not to be. What I do *will* be used by persons and groups unknown, in the predictable and sometimes violent efforts to perpetuate their own agendas in the world. I continue my work, but within such penumbras.
   Though little credit has been given or recognition tendered to the possible development of a radical self-plumbing before the beginning of the

3rd millenium BCE, recent palaeographic research yields a sense of person as self-examiner far earlier than any posited up to now. To the almost miraculous and widely recognized period which gave birth among others to the Mosaic teachings—1500 BCE, Socrates and the Buddha—500 BCE, and the Essene Christ, and their outflows, we must now add (ca. 3200 BCE) the excursions in subjectivity here-under subjoined; most probably non-Semitic, the Mind/ Texture/Determinatives whose recently discovered existence I shall reveal in the course of this laboratory teachings memoir seem ancestral to such true openings into Self as are found in St. Augustine and the Desert Fathers—in whom so many historians had previously found the founts, the early openings into self-travelling. Indeed, the perversely refulgent harmonics of the Great Sanhedrin, of the great Inquisitor Torquemada, of the great avenging presences in contemporary Teheran—undoubtedly in most polities of the present world —these harmonics infect my sleep. But work makes freedom.

I would also call attention to the power of the unsullied literary imag-ination evident in the texts which are the object of my studies, a power gen-erously evident in the work of the so-called scribes, who were of course redac-tors, a vector we usually ignore. Thus often the line between redactor and author is hard to draw.

The magnificent and hallowed pictographs which, after Falkenstein and Schmandt-Besserat, I see as only very occasionally translatable into sound values, were certainly the work of our most genial, and probably our *only* non-Semitic precursors—the *first*, Sumerian, civilization. Deep time. Without them the very scripts of the Akkadians, the Hittites, the Babylonians, the Assyrians, the Ugarits—the scripts of so many Semites, in use for more than 3,000 years, amassing an endlessly and immensely unpayable debt to the Sumerians—with-out them these systematic scripts are inconceivable. But beyond the pic-tographs, and specially as complexly articulated with them, the Mind/Texture/ Determinatives recently discovered truly reveal the nascent stages of the histo-ry of consciousness. (In the later course of these *Tablets* I shall push back this early notational frontier some 16,000 years and attempt to reveal an articula-tion. Here I present a few pictographic phrases merely at this phase of our work to acquaint the reader-looker with some of the visual forms and combi-nations.)

[Handwritten marginalia, left margin:] is this start of ... if. discovery ... human ... to plumb depths of consciousness are at an understanding ... place ... the world ... links the disparate voices of people ... use tablets ... an effort that's been on-going since the dawn of human consciousness ... (once human) became ... humans) ... aspect that ... distinguishes us from animals + it's an effort that these tablets both comment on + continue

[Handwritten marginalia, right margin top:] These tablets as our earliest document of human soul searching ('self-plumbing')

[Handwritten marginalia, right margin middle:] as it is here (the S/T himself is our redactor)

[Handwritten marginalia, right margin lower:] So here we are entering the pre-literate space of human consciousness

[Handwritten marginalia, bottom:] So: The following pictographs are the work of the 1st Sumerian civilization. They are almost purely visual (a language of images that cannot be converted into speech). A pre-cuneiform mode of expression (almost a transitional stage b/t pictures + writing — pictures that represent things /ideas directly vs. symbols that represent the word that represents the idea)

Pre-history (as history is defined)

Foregrounding language as a code (?)
Putting us in the position of an J/T
who must decipher a script. Make sense
out of (what seems like) nonsense.

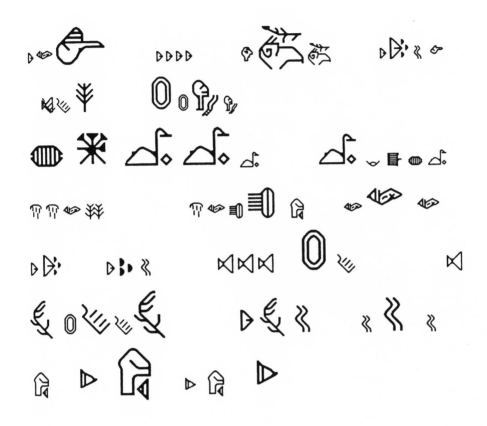

Besides a number of these representative pictographs, essentially Sumerian and pre-cuneiform, Tablet XXVI also includes Mind/Texture/Determinatives, most probably conceived by a blind Tiresias-figure who is, exceptionally for that culture, in touch with mind-texture differing strata of consciousness, a particular quality of informed subjectivity most surprising for this period in history. I have thought in this connection of Rilke's angel, "in whom space was included, as if he were blind and looking into himself." These contributions, early notations embodying archaic beginnings of human con-//sciousness, appear to be roughly contemporaneous with the earliest systematic human pictographs (although it is not clear whether the artificer *is* actually such a relatively esoteric occurence in his cultural climate, whether his contribution is an idiosyncratic conceit, a kind of gnosis, intuitive and undescribed in any available tablet or later papyrus.)

Esoteric tradition, as found only in the Tetrahedral Texts, suggests that his blindness was due to schisto-ocularia, or cleft eye, an unusual tropical disease following upon the parasitic infection Bilharziasis. Cleft eye, rarely a serious affliction since the advent of open-eye surgery, causes eventual loss of sight through the slow but inexorable development of a kind of nictitating membrane—a membrane normally present in some birds, which moves from side to side on the surface of the eye. When afflicting human beings this developmentally atavistic membrane extends itself during the slow course of the disability, from the inner corner of each eye nearest the bridge of the nose toward the other side of each of the eyes—a matter requiring generally a duration of some fifteen to seventeen years, during which perception takes on for a while somewhat the mechanism of a stereopticon.

But the object is seen as larger for only a brief while; the damage to the optic nerve has the idiosyncratic effect of doubling and miniaturizing everything in the perceptual field before sight finally fades. It is true of course that the magic lantern, or stereopticon, projects rather than perceives, but the ambiguous relationships between the M/T/D's and the pictographs puzzle the present translator in ways that often evoke the problem of the distinctions between perception and projection. The blind transformer of his private vision, whom merely for purposes of referential convenience I will name Ur-Aryan, attempts to embody his remarkable otherness in the Mind/Texture/Determinatives—we will come upon at least 15 different types, all very near each other in kind, but, as we will observe, remarkably subtly differentiated, each, it appears, indicative of a Way of Experiencing. The archetypal form of the M/T/D icon seems a highly stylized graphic whose general design may have been drawn from the traditional 4-part ruminant-stomach of various grazing quadrupeds—wisent, urus, ox and so on; existing in an other temporal layer it may also represent—a kind of palimpsest—a pictographic determinative incorporating a less detailed stomach as well as the liver and gall bladder, all of course often used in divinatory processes. Any close examination of the spatial configuration involving the liver, stomach and gall bladder of a ruminant quadruped will immediately convince the skeptic of the likely derivation of these icons.

(I reproduce the ur-form in a font-size slightly larger than the graphic pictographs clearly derived from it. Curvilinear forms characterize only a few of the very earliest pictographs. Archaic scribes, yielding to the obdurate characteristics of damp clay, very soon abandoned such forms and attempted stylized duplications of ellipse and arc by means of short lines. Incising went more quickly and with simpler reproduciblity. This technological improvement gave up the cursive. Deep time. A loss. We Gutenberg it and we're so hot for the one face of the one writer and the particularizing name):

The S/T veers off into poetry

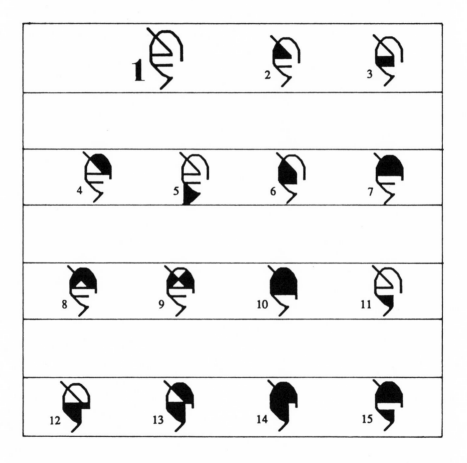

And below, approximately as seen on the one remaining wall in the lowest level at Jemdet Nasr, 162 appearances, the ur-form again, as a total utterance utterly untranslatable; we know that the 86th icon in this utterance generally represents in later periods the element Mercury and often introduces the variable of ambiguity . . . .

Obviously resulting icons such as these are as I have suggested highly stylized representations—rendered I believe by a sighted scribe doing his best to convey the artificer's inner vision in archaic graphic form. It can probably never be made clear whether the probable originator of the Determinatives had been sighted before succumbing to blindness. What puzzles me, though I am on the track of a possible solution, is the vague resemblance of the icon to a human face. We know that to many archaic peoples the stomach not the heart was the seat of feeling and thought. But—does the face equal the stomach? Or is it conceivably the gall bladder, or a hepatic lobe? The absorption of the profane by the sacred, mythical unification . . . .

Such speculations evoke Octavio Paz's intriguing comments, in one of his magistral disquisitions concerning Tantric Buddhism, about the ineffably close connections between the face and the ass, ". . . the (repressive) reality principle and the (explosive) reality principle . . . . . the metaphor both as it works upward and as it works downward—the ass a face and the face as an ass—serves each of these principles alternately.

"At first, the metaphor uncovers a similarity; then, immediately afterward, it covers it up again, either because the first term absorbs the second, or vice versa. In any case the similarity disappears and the opposition between ass and face reappears, in a form that is now even stronger than before. Here, too, the similarity at first seems unbearable to us—therefore we either laugh or cry; in the second step, the opposition also becomes unbearable—and therefore we either laugh or cry. When we say that the ass is like another face, we deny the soul-body dualism; we laugh because we have resolved the discord that we are. But the victory of the pleasure principle does not last long; at the same time that our laughter celebrates the reconciliation of the soul and the body, it dissolves it and makes it laughable again." Such Western cautions relating to many contemporary transcendental enthusiasms for imported teachings remind this writer of Jung's salutary 1952 warnings in his "Psychological Commentary" to *The Tibetan Book of the Great Liberation, or the Method of realizing Nirvana through Knowing the Mind:* "I do not doubt," he says, "that the Eastern liberation from vices, as well as from virtues, is coupled with detachment in every respect, so that the *yogi* is translated beyond this world, and quite inoffensive. *But I suspect every European attempt at detachment of being mere liberation from moral considerations."* (my italics.)

Tablet XXVI, as well as most of the materials following it, seems to embody the beginnings of early though incomplete and dualistically stained adventures into the nature of Self, the figure of that Self, flawed because in its subjectivity the ego as a dualistically reflective subject does not have access to itself as subject; its access to itself is always unavoidably as an object; the ego is separated and cut off from itself. But the impressive power of insight and the graphic incarnations of states of being, as it were of Hosts, embodied in the M/T/D's, and variously juxtaposed with different combinations and permutations of pictographs, make essential inroads into the mystery. As instances:

or

That is, in (a.) total emptiness is equal to total filling, however many individual segments are involved, and no matter what their relative sizes. In (b.) we see what seems to be a simple additive process; however further investigation into the nature and function of the first icon in reference

(b.) , will reveal its idiosyncratic use as an instrument of transformation in the majority of expressions in which it appears.

The most painful aspect of this editing process consists of the fact that inscriptions, language, forms unroll in time; only a massive graphic large enough to accomodate this entire *Tablet,* a painting obviating time, could ameliorate my desperate spiritual hiccuping, the painful manifestation of my unappeasable desire to lay it all out at once.

For a more complex example we take the following instance from this *Tablet,* XXVI, drawn from the sequence of pictographic phrases rendered above; Mind/Texture/Determinatives sometimes follow such sequences, sometimes precede them. The phrases under question contain as far as I can discern no transitional, prepositional, conjunctive or subordinating elements, no apparent inflections except maybe those of hope. Imagine the openness of the pre-inflective!

Believing strongly in the moral imperative of sharing the process of cognizing and translation with my readers in the course of presenting archaic gestures, and persisting in that belief in the face of possible misunderstanding and boredom, I now reunite some of the pictographic phrases with their common adjuncts, sometimes general <u>Mind/Texture/Determinatives</u>, sometimes Spharagrams—<u>from the Sanskrit *sphara,* 'extensive,'</u> related to Latin *spatium,* 'space,' and Skt. *sphayati,* 'increase,' 'grow fat,' akin to 'speed'—a neologism I have on appropriate occasions preferred to the somewhat long-winded term Mind/Texture/Determinative.

Before setting on Spharagram to denote an aspect of mind-work I shall soon present, I conceived of the term Sphayatigram, which I abandoned because of a lack of euphony and overhanging tinkles of obesity which would have skewed the true intent of the term as I understand it.

The Spharagram I think of in moments of linguistic and acculturative desperation as a counterpoise to my frustrating efforts to digest the true significance and function of the riverish shiftings of the M/T/D's, sometimes all mouthings, occasionally fat deltas, not so rarely arising from the source headlands of undescriable thought-mountain sources. A very hell of a natural wonder in fact.

The <u>Mind/Texture/Determinative has complex attributes;</u> occasionally it implies <u>benign,</u> or <u>transformative,</u> or <u>restorative functions;</u> sometimes it represents <u>negative aspects of the general precognitive substratum,</u> which represents the ground within which a specific utterance occurs. Let us take as

an instance the phrase cited above: ⬤▤ ▤◖ or earth/*ki*, great/*gal*, fire/*izi.*

When the Mind/Texture/Determinative ⬡ completes the phrase, as in

⬤▤◖ ⬡ , the sequence: midsize-<u>earth</u> + midsize <u>great</u> + proportionally large <u>fire</u> usually = oneness, at-homeness, ease-in-dwelling, large-acceptance,

from the usual meaning of ▤◖ as fire or sunlight scorching to a final one-

81

ness, unity, particularly when the icon, relatively enlarged, is used in terminal position. But when the sequence is completed by the M/T/D ᛫, the significance changes radically, given the usual meaning of this determinative: **egocentric demandingness.** What has been called the "behind" quality of mind, inert, heavy, viscous, hot, subject to internalizing fortification and hatred, part of the pervasive texture of experience, is an aspect most characteristic of many M/T/D's, and rare evidence of archaic iconic representation of complex internal states. In this case the phrase under consideration signifies not ease-in-dwelling or unity but rather profound homelessness, tendency to attack neighbors, irremediable sadness leading to the sort of inner heat that consumes not warms. Certain human attributes—fury; envy; unselective appetite; contempt; unbridled ambition; massive despair; unboundaried self-pity; terror; pleasure at the exercise, however apparently benign, of power; overeating—all carry powerful characteristics of this "behind" quality of mind.

Much has been written about the *dépaysement,* the *heimatlos* condition of the present world experience. It is thus of the greatest interest to have discovered in these materials from Jemdet Nasr not merely ancient progenitors of ultimate loss but immediate relatives.

The Spharagrams include Determinatives which particularly emphasize the aspects of openhandedness, freshness, clarity, trusting but not oafish confidence, generosity unaddled by mental soup. (The categorization is instrumental not hard and fast. One scholar's spharagram may be another's M/T/D fumble.) Thus the phrase ᛫᛫᛫᛫᛫ , literally: *clarity/opening-out/giving health/recognition of the object,* + vulvar pictographs signifying woman, = *garden, world-vulva, heavy-liquid-of-becoming, power.* The Spharagram itself does not *indicate* or itself contain the knowledge of the how of consciousness development, but it opens a vector and opens spaces for one's realization of such knowledge as the looker/reader does his practice through the text. Deep space. Thus the icon is part of a symbolic system not altogether unlike musical notation, which alters and interprets the ground of human performance, in this case not merely linguistic but through and across the bridge of the linguistic and symbolic—fully appreciating and going beyond cognition by means of experience.

Before presenting the first of a number of extant versions of *Tablet XXVI,* I now consider a few more examples of the ambiguities and amusing perversities which the translation of these materials entails. Take for instance the expression:

What is the nature of the implied relationship between M/T/D terms 1 and 14 in this phrase? We have already seen that 1) *clarity/opening-out/giving-health* is the ur–Spharagram. We know from intense linguistic research, and we have seen, that in

total emptiness, opening-out, seems in a few expressions functionally equal to *totally filled,* however many individual segments are involved, and no matter what their relative sizes. The lack of logic embodied in this lopsided equation seems to me to require further examination, all the more because I am drawn in by some shadow of conviction informing the relationship among the factors, a shadow that seems to me not to deserve serious consideration. Often what can be initially experienced as an entertainment, as in this case, continues as a sadness. I cannot open the inner knot. If I could get into the space between the icons I could know something, say as if living inside Mozart's music, find a fact about distances, about the nature of the M/T/D reciprocals 1 and 14—converse or supplement.

The boundaried expression presented earlier on,
is in some extant versions the initial, medial or penultimate segment of Tablet

XXVI and gives us *earth/great/fire* + *earth/great/fire* + *earth/great/fire* + *star/god* + *mouth.* A straightforward reading might yield the sense,

In the great ease-in-dwelling, in the large acceptance, in the oneness,
In the at-homeness, the constellation (米米米) which is the god
Lives within the boundary, within the voice, separated but near
Separated from the man's house, the woman's great lit house,
Separated + + + + + and so near the woman's earth, the man's great fire
Near and separate from the fire/sun scorching into unity
The great land, the house, the great woman and the man, the great
Dwelling in the recognized ease of the great lit earth
In the utterance of the person at the end of the incised clay trail
Which is the wake of the trail of the great lit land & house & the god
And the voice.

Where is he, mouth of the ear

extrapolating sense from symbols whose meaning, logic are totally unknown to him.

Great artificer . . . . , perturbed basket of claims
Shoot of shoots & shrinker of [retinues]
Making the mazy watery blue one oozing red
Entreating stutterer in the meaning cave
When they ask Whose, your back curves the answer
In a lion's bending . . . . of a mongoose
Where is he seedling tribulation mixer in the fat ground
Jewel testicle of the mouth & listener, great ear of the mouth
& self-abused leader in the brief low mind mushroom constellations
Quickly unforming to black ooze & rot & stringy filth
Separated and so near the woman's earth, the man's great fire
Near and separate from the fire/sun scorching into unity

The earliest appearance of the extract above excludes determinatives, one of which, in each of four later versions, appears in a crucial position and of a qualifying size, and, within the focus of a certain kind of consideration, puts into question the essential direction of this entire text, which seems to concern itself with the figure we have identified above as the blind transformer, the ur-Aryan, the artificer. Tablet XXVI, we will observe in the course of our work together, includes little hymns of departure, ambiguous lilts of arrival, putative transmogrifications, grievous insult apostrophes, paeans and dirges. We find the variant,

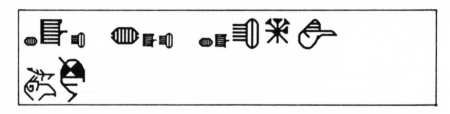

in which the M/T/D: , number 9, refers to *symmetry, loss of energy, stasis, death*. (To recapitulate, compare this icon with the two spharagrams

1   14   and the three M/T/D's we have so far encountered:

2   , 5   and 9   referring, in the given order—briefly—to processes of Transformation; Egocentric Demandingness; and Radical Loss of Energy.)

Most remarkably, the variant phrase given above contains a singular instance of an M/T/D-blocker; that is, when any Mind/Texture/Determinative is preceded by the following untranslatable pictograph:

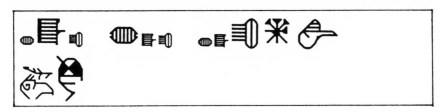 , apparently a face looking up at a branchlet of some sort, that Determinative is totally neutralized, as if a charge in an electrical field had been electrochemically held to absolute balance within all particles. <u>Of course all analogies break down</u>, and I do not mean to press this one too far. It will serve as suggestion of force field activity. Thus to return to the variant phrase,

no change occurs in its meaning. Why in this case was the Determinative not simply left out? Many languages manifest unreasonable conservative fixations, the *gh* for the sound *F* in English, the *spr* for the sound *T* in Tibetan and so forth, *sprulku* sounded *tulku* for instance. This may be a somewhat similar persistence. However, it may be that an unknown redactor of *Tablet XXVI,* potentially encumbered by whatever eventual socio-religious repercussions he might have envisaged and feared, intended to void a significant semantic alteration of the text. Unfortunately, we do not know the circumstances or the provenance of even the first change in the phrase, which itself originally presented the Determinative.

We have however recovered the four following sub-variants,

aa.

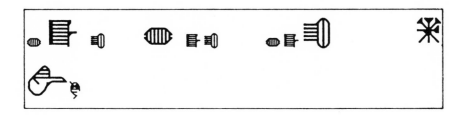

bb.

cc.

dd.

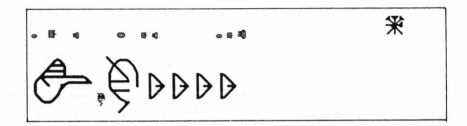

what are we to make of these instances?

In the first sub-variant, *aa*, all pictographs have withered, being barely recognizable:

aa.

Ironically, given the down cast of this version, these pictographs are among the most finely incised examples of any surviving work on clay. Little ambiguity attends *aa*. Cognate inscriptions and the logic of the linguistic and historical circumstance lead me to believe that we have in *aa.* the following, completed by a number of lines presented above:

He is already dead. He has died. The ease-in-dwelling atrophies + + + + + + + +
Separated, small, risible, voiceless . . . . ridiculous, filiform, dry,
The blackened fire & the whitened earth swallowed like the stupid greatness
Of the helpless constellation, the house and the memories of water,
The chastened mouth, the dismembered voice + + + + + + + + + + + +
The boundaries are lost in the . . . . , the sepulcher of the no-memory
Of the moles & saliva & lost fingernail-parings & the dried eyeballs
Stare not even seeing the nothing of everything, they are absent
To themselves, juiceless, blind staring mad. Husk. Rabid in death.
            Where is he, mouth of the ear
Great artificer, perturbed basket of claims
Shoot of shoots & shrinker of [retinues]
Making the mazy watery blue one oozing red
Entreating stutterer in the meaning cave . . . . + + + + + + + + +
When they ask Whose, his back curves the answer, proud execution
Of a lion's back dancing . . . . of a mongoose bending a snake
"As if in my stomach," he would say, right hand by his mouth & voice
No mere picture making on the cave wall
            Where is he seedling tribulation mixer in the fat ground
Jewel testicle of the mouth & listener, great ear of the mouth
& self-abused leader in the brief low mind [mushroom] constellations
Quickly unforming to black ooze & rot & stringy filth
Separated and so near the woman's earth, the man's great fire in
+ + + + + + + + + + + + + + ... + + + + + + + + + + + + + + + ++ + + + + + + +
So near and separate and far from the fire/sun scorching into unity.

To avoid unnecessary and possibly tiring duplication and repetition I shall present all translations of the three remaining sub-variant segments in succession; I shall dispense with an overly detailed analysis of my translation process in this case; the attentive reader-looker may at his leisure work out the correspondences. And I remind him that I do not indicate lost or partly obliterated passages in these representative pictographic sketches, although I may include them in my translations. (Variants *cc.* and *dd.*, incised separately upon the last remaining wall at Jemdet Nasr, are directly followed by the untranslateable 162-unit spharagram-constellation reproduced above.)

Briefly, the burdens of the sub-variants *bb, cc, dd*, indicate the following:

bb. He is not quite dead (pictograph f, *mouth*, increases a bit in size at the expense of M/T/D *9, symmetry/loss of energy/death/stasis.*)

bb.

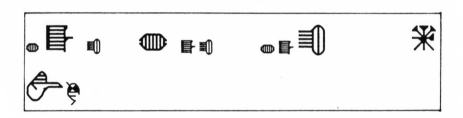

cc. He is someone else, perhaps an animal (M/T/D 2, Spharagram of Transformation, overcoming the somewhat shrunken M/T/D of symmetry and death and loss of energy, completes the phrase here.)

cc.

dd. He will surely never die (The pictographic molecule, *heavy-liquid-of-becoming; power, world-vulva,* (⟨image⟩) is added to complete the phrase; in addition we now find between the pictographs *star/god* and *mouth,* pictographs *i* and *u* representing *sun/early morning* (⟨image⟩) in conjunction

with the pictograph *childbirth,* (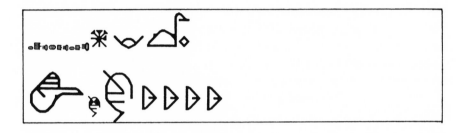) a very powerful intensive, also under–
standable as *great-eye-of-light* and *birth-bird,* both extant in a joint presentation in
one other appearance at Ras Shamra, with the signification *birth-giving-eye-
which-fuses-opposites-through-holy-scorching-and-which-blinds-for-seeing.*)

dd.

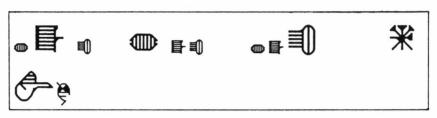

He is not quite dead. Between the star and mouth
The abyss sucks the tiny winging desert flies to dry death and also
Between the great fire
And star in the forlorn symmetry of the beautiful.
     The <u>blind artificer</u> said:

When I was young they would praise
just about all I'd say, as if I breathed
with them; my times are bad, the past is a joke,
former admirers hound me, alone and treed

what's left of my ties with them who
praised anything out of my mouth—my voice
now that life floors me and they cut
my best song, seeing what, lies?

what we had together is lost; they praised me once
for any language at all; I'm now to fall,
now in my troubles; my merit is my seeing,
their hate infects my days

I was acclaimed; whatever came
deserved their praise; now hostage to my life
I encounter their contempt for my dearest
song; I live in loss and strife.

they laugh at the breath I love—
once, whatever I voiced, they'd give me
praises; my life now in a painful
fall, what do they see?

is nothing left? my friends and my time
have turned on me who once
was the target for praise: the oracle
turns dunce.

what we had I was
acclaimed what I love has turned dearest hostage
any words at all
out of my liver; what I gave I gave
with my mouth from the inside
of my eyes now that life floors
I encounter anything their need for the fall grain
is nothing young? they praised as I breathed
my times are with them the past is treed, alone I said
which dunce was the target for which oracle?
admirer's a joke bitterness
a dunce the hound of the empty is the full,

                    was what we lost
what we had?
now my best lies in the cut of my trouble every target
deserves work **beauty**
is the purgation
of superfluities

In this stony ground of the great artificer,
In the holes, between mountains . . . . hot . . . .
Wild bulls compose themselves in his breath which is the hot wind
Of the desert of his words but also in his bitter word-trap he is
Inhospitable to lost cows and goats, brutal to the lost. Where
Is the room in him for the tame, the life of milk and riverrun fields,
Overcome as he totters over the cave of his stomach holding his words,
Great carpenter of the insides.
                    The sweet language waters grow
From his stomach, ... his + + + + + + + +, his . . . .
From his testicles, and in his heart the semen grows
Into the fetus-form of his [verbs.] That kill him in a great fire
Separated from a house. That will sicken him in a vast house
Cut away from the life of flames and scorching. He goes. May he die.
He leaves. May he die. We will continue + + + + + + + + + + + + + + + + + +
In the bleached world. He dies.
We will store what even his greed can not curb. Still riddles pierce us.
He is who? A she. Giving out. Leaping in. Cut away and thinning out. Deep
Song. Great shaken word-stuff + + + + + + + + + missing + + + + + + + + ...
Leaving a change. The abyss is a hope
Yawning between mouth and star.
                    The barley of his words
Swells in the wrong ground of his liver, the child of his verbs puffs up
In the wrong field of his sickening heart, he is wrong in body

equating language
w/ landscape

91

For this bearing, he is shaken . . . . + + + + + + + + + + +
As in the pitiless beak of a gliding
Vulture over his own stony ground, the rock-words of his hot tenancy
Themselves overcome in the trial, he falls + + + + + + + + + + + +
Mushroom dark [spider]
In the filiform sadness of his heart's thin remaining afterbirth language
After his perverse gift, his rain,
In the near-death and the blind rise of his word-fall happiness.

cc.

He is someone else, perhaps an animal. He lives inside plant names.
He races inside his messages of fleet means. He is the calling voice
Of the names inside the wheat and the barley. He can't say them
Forever. He tells them +
Through the inside of his eyes, he sees
The inside of his eyes and describes the animal names of plants.
He looks and tells. He lives inside the scorching sun, he also leans
+ + + + + + + + + upwards + + + + + + + + + downwards + + + + + ...
In his long trial toward the sun
. . . . the name of the water falling, the voice
In the water slithering and trekking underneath the soil calling
To receive the good names, to say the good names, and to receive
And to receive . . . . like the king of the hurricane who draws
Lightning and + the sound, the proper
Voice for the saying, the murmuring, the uttering, the chant
Of wheat and barley changed by murmur into animal liveliness,
By uttering, by striking the stomach and opening the . . . .

dd.

<u>*He will surely never die.*</u> <u>The world is made of his voice.</u>

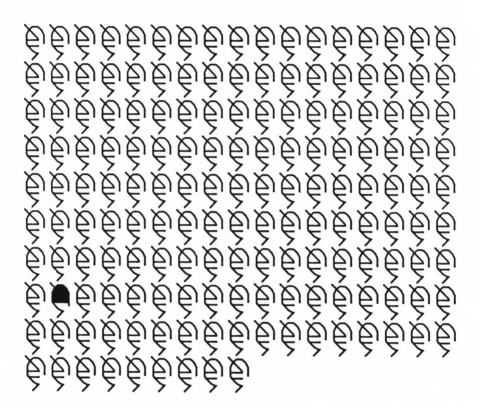

       Where is he, mouth of the ear
Great artificer, perturbed basket of claims
Shoot of shoots & shrinker of [retinues]
Making the mazy watery blue one oozing red
Entreating the stutterer in the meaning cave . . . . + + + + + + + +
When they ask Whose, his back curves the answer, proud execution
Of a lion's back dancing . . . . of a mongoose bending a snake
"As if in my stomach," he would say, right hand by his mouth & voice

No mere picture making on the cave wall
       Where is he seedling tribulation mixer in the fat ground
Jewel testicle of the mouth & listener, great ear of the mouth
& self-abused leader in the brief low mind [mushroom] constellations
Quickly unforming to black ooze & rot & stringy filth
Separated and so near the woman's earth, the man's great fire in
+ + + + + + + + + + + + + + ... + + + + + + + + + + + + + + + + + + +
So near and separate and far from the fire/sun scorching into unity.

      To the degree that I am involved in the process of formation of the canon of this sacred material, and to the degree that I will be responsible for the slamming of the gates to any future inclusions, I have experienced a certain resistance against the placement of the segment "Where is he, mouth of the ear . . ." after the affecting brevity of variant *dd* and the monumental presence of the 162 Jemdet Nasr cave wall graphics. I tend to think that in the interest of their teachings earlier redactors might very possibly have omitted the rhetorically diffusing movement following such an inspirational apotheosis. But palaeography is not propaganda.

TABLET XXVII

From the Laboratory-Teachings-Memoirs of the Scholar/Translator

Nine closely related clay Cylinder-Seals constitute Tablet XXVII.

A thin sheet of clay measuring about 54 inches by 4 inches was rolled to produce a cylinder 54 by 1, then cut into approximately 9 equal lengths, inscribed and fired. Electron microscopy of the cylinder ends testifies to this structural origin of the Seals; it does not absolutely guarantee the congruence of the materials. These documents, with the exception of number 1, are dilapidated.

They are the only ones extant whose structure can to any degree be conceived of as narrative; they do not much resemble other seals—generally devices used as a means of marking property not recounting Story. In addition they are remarkable for their startling linguistic formations, idiosyncratically arranged combinations of Akkadian cuneiform and pictographic Sumerian, archaizings, rare reshufflings which forcibly anneal these two different writing systems, their periods separated by hundreds of years. I will never forget the vibrations, the shimmerings, that overmastered me when, my arm outstretched, I first experienced the pressure of one of these Seals on the palm of my left hand.

I had to consider a number of factors in the course of the difficult and engaging process of naming the language-constructions inscribed on these Seals: to what degree do the inscriptions fulfill the requirements which the category "language" & imposes as a condition of membership? These unique presentations may result from the labors of a small group, perhaps even from those of one individual. The idiosyncratic utterance-combinations inscribed on these Seals contain, to repeat, in varied arrangements, both pictographic and cuneiform expressions, as well as innovative diacritical inscriptions.

I indicated in Tablet XXVI Laboratory-Teachings-Memoirs my experience of some interesting problems, both phonic and categorical, in arriving at acceptable names for such terms as Spharagram and Mind/Texture/Determinative. Names matter; they suggest directions for later research; they convey texture which influences further scholarly speculation. My original term for the language-constructions in Tablet XXVII, "pictocunei," rhythmic cripple, was one of those terms whose barely semi-resident status in the English language the unabridged dictionaries indicate; in my second attempt,

96

"cuneopicts," the constant cluster, now massively terminal, conveyed the image of an early golden-haired Brit at his ravaging work. I came finally to choose the less literal, euphonious, more complexly relevant term, "ominacunei." The Latin "omina" signifies in the nominative plural both "forebodings" and "signs"; thus, besides its stress on the representational attributes of the pictograph, this first element in the neologism "*omina* cunei"—apprehending, dark, gravid, premonitory—connotes the parturition of the pictograph, which eventuated in the alphabet.

Some of the writings preserved through these Cylinder-Seals are essentially later rescissions of some lines from Tablet IX, itself an opaque document bearing here and there, speckles of a secret ritual language, a not unusual linguistic feature seen for instance in such gatherings as those of the Inuit peoples collected in the course of Rasmussen's Thule Expeditions. These extraordinarily large Seals, which as we have seen average some six inches in length and one inch in diameter, thus seem to constitute an exoteric version of an esoteric original. My sense of the Seals as entropic narrative rests upon a series of implications derived from the idiosyncratic determinatives first seen in these contexts.

I might say more accurately that these specialized forms function not like the Mind/Texture/Determinatives which we have encountered in Tablet XXVI, but rather like Stage Directors, or let's say like what I will name Utterance/Texture/Indicators (U/T/I's), which isolate particular vectors largely related to the External World Stage and graft them onto a written expression. Members of the U/T/I family differ from those included in the M/T/D set in ways at once profound and illusory, an apparent paradox which will receive some clarification in the course of these Laboratory-Teachings-Memoirs. I could add though that contemporary speculation often conceives the Mind/Texture/Determinatives as referring to states of being—whose idiosyncratic natures beg for recognition. They also hunger for responses of individuals potentially victimized by any negative energies of such states. Thus the genesis of the M/T/D's derives from survival-needs, from the hunger to see clearly, without impediment. (A major problem of course is that, following Kant, we understand that it is precisely impedimenta to clear-seeing of a thing-as-such which linguistic forms as reflectors of consciousness commonly embody. Rather than a game of Who or What do you trust?, it seems to be a question of What is real? Not evaluation but flat-out thereness.) The U/T/I's facilitate in some sense an ongoing Exodus from the esoteric utterances of Tablet IX. They constitute in some senses the external social analogues of the M/T/D's textures and functions. Graphic representations, forthcoming, will clarify these matters.

The U/T/I *leads* the esoteric original into the demotic realm, a space that may have resulted from an attempt—through a sort of anachronistic reconstruction—to present a Golden Age whose lineaments parallel aspects of later periods.

We might with a greater chance of accuracy understand such linguistic inventions as *sacred forgery*, or rather forgery prompted by a dazzled and mournful reconsideration, retrospective as well as perhaps economically profitable, of the sacred. I will translate and comment upon some of the Seals, in a few cases presenting original phrases found in Tablet IX followed by their later rescensions, each often generated through the fascinating and unexampled use of sub-orders of major Utterance/Texture/Indicators. My reader is advised to conceive of the U/T/I's as aspects of the Mind/Texture/Determinatives presented in Tablet XXVI, although the U/T/I's behave more like vectors of a sociocultural, demographic order than they do like descriptors relating to subjective states of being. They somewhat parallel the nature of the M/T/D's, but often depend for their meaning upon an intuitive familiarity with the ways human and other animal bodies can occupy space, and they often operate like a kind of uncanny, Body-Mind Declension calling to mind the recent work of Birdwhistell and Eshkol-Wachmann, the speculations of Effort-Shape analysts.

The maker, or makers, of the Seals focused upon the pictographic, immanent thereness explicit in the nascent pictures of what he or *they* knew as the mirroring gem of the old systematic representations; the makers moved thence into the juxtaposition of two inscribed systems, one image and archaism, the other drawn directly from the Akkadian cuneiform.

What was the nature of the attempt? Perhaps to recoup the powers of the past without the sacrifice of the present—instinct with the knowledge of the doom attendant upon any creative thrust which thumbed its nose at its own time. This tendency, earning its own defeat, would fall into the constraining and reductive hell of either/or.

In the example

This represents the position of the solitary reader in relation to a text.

the Broken-Scissor Utterance/Texture/Indicator, U/T/I of Solitary Reading

and Subsuming Position-determinative, 𝄞 , alerts the perceiver of the utterance—solitary reader in a private space—that he is to imagine himself as acting in the context of a specific Body-Declension which, as we will see below, is to follow the Broken-Scissor U/T/I, establishing through this practice a connection with the utterance which sometimes ranges, in a three-state continuum, from a state of disinterested observation to one of profound and wounding separation from the object-phrase. (The icons representing these three stages, as well as those denoting ways of occupying space, will be given below.)

The function of this U/T/I concerns performance and relationship, not the reification of an isolation threatening to enshroud a solitary reader faced with a "text." Although we generally conceive of that reader as separated from the dance and music ordinarily associated with archaic and tribal modes of "poetry," it's a common and insistent mistake to envision the post-archaic world as the site of increasing numbers of civilized sad troglodytes existing in a hell of separatism and loss. The rites and poetry/music/dance didn't end. They entered mind.

The pictograph, swollen, textured and laminated by the very tracks of its past forms, had kept itself vivid through its stratigraphic development, in the long moment of its extended historical playing field, occasionally as palimpsest, the simultaneity of performance and sign. (Tablet XXVII presented states of the early graphic development of the pictograph, in the context of such divinatory materials as quadruped livers, stomachs and gall bladders.)

relating to the classification + interpretation of stratified rock

Three sample utterances will suggest the nature of the infra-determinatives governing the reader's Dream-Generation of Body-Declensions—to which I will append a partial sign-list derived from the Cylinder-Seals. Both the determinative-family and the rather broad-based characteristics of design variables begin to be apparent:

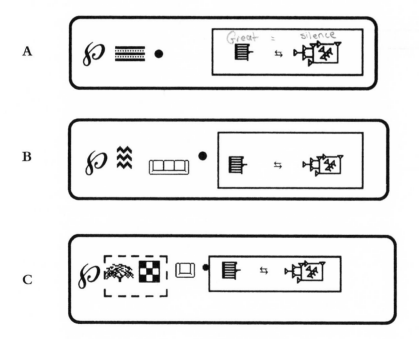

In each of these three instances the core expression consists of two segments, a pre-Sumerian pictograph signifying "great," which has already appeared in Tablet XXVI, indissolubly allied with a variant of Akkadian cuneiform signifying "silence." The pictographic elements will be presented as white on a black ground when they weigh at least twice as much as the conjoined cuneiform segments.

The cuneiform sign 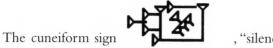, "silence," derives from two

elements, "mouth," , with "harvest," or "grain," as an

infix. Thus, A   B   C:

<u>"Silence is the harvest of the mouth."</u>
"Silence is the harvest of the mouth."
"Silence is the harvest of the mouth."

Introducing and modifying the core expression, the infra-determinatives follow the Broken-Scissor Utterance/Texture/Indicator in Cylinder-Seal 1 and denote the source physical position from which a reader/looker relates to the affective and logical aspects of an expression. So the infra-determinatives

following directly upon the subsuming symbol constitute a kind of instrumental case eliciting in the isolated reader Dreamed Body-Declensions within which, or through the agency of which, he or she may experience the phrase-object and its harmonics. Utterances B and C, above, contain examples of two specialized U/T/I's, moments of force of Separativeness, or Torques of Separativeness; three exist:

These Torques indicate—in intensifying measures of the experience of Otherness—<u>the intensity of separation which most appropriately qualifies the space between the reader and the object-phrase</u>. Such U/T/I's can be considered as occupying a middle ground between pure Mind/Texture/Determinatives and pure U/T/I's, neither Primarily reflexive nor pointedly sociological, however focused on the human body as vector working the space between person and community.

But three other elements which are present in utterances A, B and C modify the core expressions which follow them:

In A,

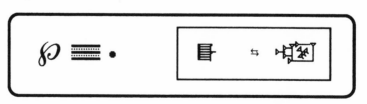

the sign signifies the reader's Dream-Generation of the Body-Declension "lying-down dying." Now, seen through a first, literal, simple step into translation, utterance A moves towards:

"In my ending, prone, I inhabit the great silence,

harvest of the mouth,"

or

"In my ending, prone, I inhabit the silence, great

harvest of the mouth,"

or

"In my ending, prone, I inhabit the silence,

the grains, the great mouth."

Of course a disproportionately heavy pictograph—here a white image on black ground—in any of the *ominacunei*, may radically alter the manner in which the entire utterance is conceived. In such an instance

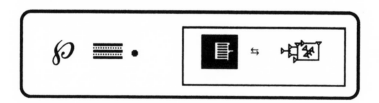

Greatly inhabiting
my ending, prone, I myself
great harvest
great mouth
silence
great

In B, the sign signifies the reader's Dream-Generation of the Body-Declension "crouched dying"; in addition the utterance contains the highest Torque of Separativeness:

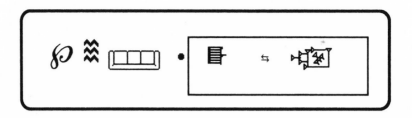

In a first reading, then,

> "In my crouched dying, I am sundered
> from the great silence,"

                                                    or

> "Immured in my crouch,
> in my dying, barred, dis-
> connected, arms hopeless, cracked
> legs, there is only
> away—not quite the memory
> of a strain towards great
> silence,"

        or

> "Going, impassable, heaviest world
> of distance between me
> and the harvest of the great
> mouth, no
> silence, pincered body so, dusk,
> carries so
> much."

In C, the sign signifies the reader's Dream-Generation of the
Body-Declension "Lying down giving birth":

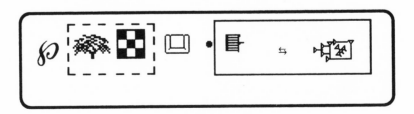

(That a part of this icon seems to portray a deciduous tree, although a surprising choice, is not without some environmental appropriateness. Both Sessile and Syrian oaks grew in what is now Syria; in present Iraq large open oak forests were found on the Zagros mountains at altitudes of between 2000 and 6000 feet.)

Translation here involves apprehending (ad/prehendere, to seize, to go towards in seizing), yielding to mimetic triggers, being led therefrom into Sympathy-Meditation through kernel-things. The best is to read "what was never written, the most ancient reading before all languages"; second best is the earned arrival at an "impeccable naïveté," escape from system, which is "a kind of damnation which forces us into a perpetual recantation" of any faith in the possibility of the rebirth of the pristine eye.

Simplistic analogues of the Body-Declension "Lying-Down-Giving-Birth" attracted the barbs of jejune flower-children on the trendy watch in the 1960s. It is nevertheless true that in comparison with the archaic, communally sanctioned Body-Declension "Crouching-Giving-Birth," the former does constitute under historic Gallic auspices a gracile aristocratic insertion into tradition—a kind of elegance at odds with the benign vector of the force of gravity; in addition the utterance contains the first Torque of Separativeness. Separated from whom, from what, how sharply?

My study of this utterance convinces me that it concerns rather than a woman a male Priest of Sacrifices. The perverse melody of exodus which this sequence emits recalls a section of its esoteric paradigm in Tablet IX, a document probably the confession—in extremis and partly notated in a secret language—of unsuccessful sacrifical denudations:

"... it is
never enough, I've surrendered the damp lips of speech
emptied these eye sockets filled my ears with good clay, ground down
my fingertips I'm left like a dog to smell my way to the dream
THIS IS AN EMPTYING . . . . so much living . . . ."

The difficulty posed by utterance C derives to some degree from the confounding or conflation of gender and gender function; but the expression is most marked by a great effort at exoteric clarification of its original, indwelling, conflict—the rift between the Way of Expressing and the Way of the Creation-Hunger, the search for the unexampled, one of the earliest instances extant of the proliferating panzer mind-track of the contemporary West.

We remind ourselves at this juncture in our task, and we take joy from it, we insist upon it—the grounding fact and enveloping determinant of Body in this domain. The Body-Declension categories, the Broken-Scissor U/T/I of Solitary Reading and Subsuming Position-determinative, the Torques of Separativeness, embody such power that in a recent instance of the rare appearance in Zurich of a text somewhat parallel to the objects of our study, a text which had retained only the U/T/I's and M/T/D's, the mere examination of the formal sequence elicited from a Swiss linguist a fugue of uncontrollable weeping.

All of the Cylinder-Seals under consideration are unusually large, a fortunate attribute in the light of their very poor condition. We are left barely enough to work from. Unlike Seal 1, none offers an absolutely clear sequence, though such can be intuited. Because they. suffer from worm borings, pilferage and bad breaks, they pose a powerful challenge to artists engaged in epigraphic reconstruction. In fact comminuted fractures at various points in these Seals occasionally left discoverers facing small fractals of dust intruding upon the horizontal continuities of the archaic leftovers.

The archeological layer which yielded our Cylinder-Seals also contained an early- and pre-cuneiform sign-list; its location right by the Seals, the idiosyncratic attributes of the signs, as well as the results of Carbon-14 dating, render it particularly relevant as a trove of the contemporary language. Although I strongly suspect the list was inscribed by the same hand as that of the Seals, a sense of my limitations imposed by the idiosyncratic texture of the material impelled me to seek for an energetic translation; I chose for the work Brad De Lisle, a young scholar in whom I saw a veritable double for my youthful self! His aesthetic pertinacity and research energy seemed to me suited to the task.

Because of the parlous state of the Cylinder-Seals, de Lisle suggested the following procedure: we would present whatever Seal utterances remained viable as found *in situ*, present a selected glossary of Body-Declension, pictographic, cuneiform and any other relevant terms and then (profiting also from the availability of the early materials found in the same archeological bed) we would present his synoptic translation. I concurred and added the suggestion,

which he accepted, that we use the icon of the Departing Man, 🚶 , to indicate missing Seal segments; he insisted that his translation practice proceed through the Path of Sympathy-Meditation.

[handwritten margin, top left:] There is no such thing as emotional distance in scholarship (though that is the accepted guise)

[handwritten margin, bottom left:] w/out even realizing it, the S/T has transformed his works from scholarship into his own idiosyncratic poetry. More than anything else, these are documents of his own subjective vision.

104

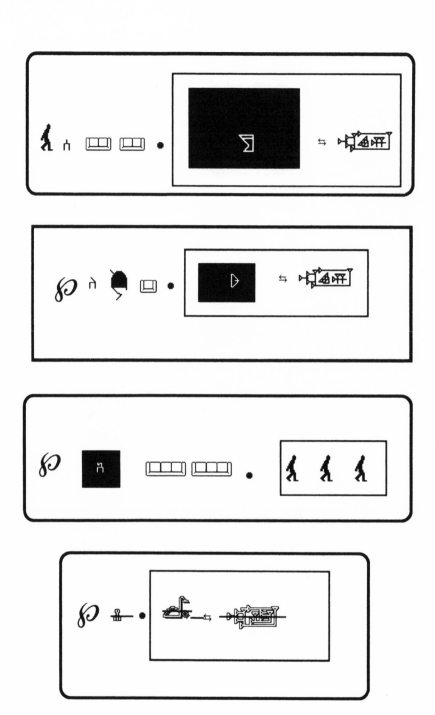

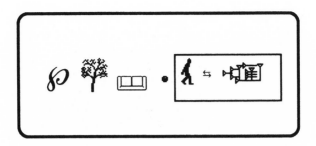

GLOSSARY:

Body-Declensions:

Standing: ☥

Lying Down: ↳

Seated: ☥

Lying Down Sick: 🌳

Crouched: ⋔

Lying Down Giving Birth:

Crouched Sick: ⋔

Lying Down Shitting:

Crouched Giving Birth: ⋔

Lying Down Dying: ▤

Crouched Shitting: ⋀

Boundaryless Identification: ↰

Crouched Dying: ≋

SELECTED PICTOGRAPHS APPEARING IN CYLINDER-SEALS 1-9

EAT:

FOOD:

HAND:

PENIS:

WOMAN:

CHILDBIRTH:

M/T/D of AMBIGUITY:

Cuneiform Signs:

Mouth:

Father/Exorcist: = Mouth +

Father + determinative following names of fish

Spittle/Venom/Saliva: = Mouth +

To curse, malediction, a desire

Rebellion: 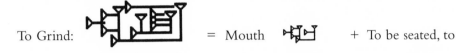 = Mouth ⟦cuneiform⟧ + Ishkur, the God Adad, god of tempest, determinative preceding the name of the four cardinal points ⟦cuneiform⟧

To Grind: ⟦cuneiform⟧ = Mouth ⟦cuneiform⟧ + To be seated, to find oneself, to live in a certain place, one's home, basic place, root ⟦cuneiform⟧

To Roar/Bellow/Resonate/Re-echo: ⟦cuneiform⟧ = Mouth +

To Count, Recite; Account; Recitation ⟦cuneiform⟧

Derived Sympathy-Meditation Song:

shine atttempted birth of closed regions
and fall in slave incantations plentitude—
cut honey, separate silence and anus, web grains
for pregnancy conduct of a great mouth a
lost harvest, palsy, & sweet
stress of muscle fear to burn
gather exudae in a quiet
& swear tomorrow
for talk better talk sadder
mouths of loud grains
unassailable & sad, teeth.
It's a dream-brother pain opening
or worse, quiet slows, violation by zephyr
& I lying down giving & sadder
will leave anus-silence foundations,
sweet barriers, & I collecting and
loss, and harvest, and velvet palsy playing like home.
be somber little breast, man's entrails play world,
taking leave
universe-clay is one & destroy closed regions
as cleaver be as cleaver
belly as quiet SLOWS, defending to excite and even despair
of losses from all scribe violence attempted, longed-for & lamented

terror-paces.
Are leavetakings to exacerbate the wishing-sense, the
lovely sweet *ahead* in an anger/turn, corkscrew-hunger
to pullulate tender wastes of action, hands sowing in air but cut
cut, cut off at the desire-notch, it feels
small boy-belly as cleaver, what's pierceable &
equal to the grow in losing, wet meaning, desire
conflated with loss & fusion—
O Desire: wash praise wash prisoner, take & wash, you, picture &
prisoner of the eye, fistula for opening
father epilepsy venom, leave be there windlift

Waking up from my dream seems about the same as being inside it. The lower half of my body is mired in some sort of holdfast earthworks, in spite of which my 49 pair of legs tread in a fluid language as if protectively cloistered in a viscous embrace; my torso, very long and straining towards the sunlight, is punctured by seven clean holes, the diameter of the posterior exit wounds two to three times that of the anterior holes, which expand conically. Floating on an aircushion above the neutral ocean, I easily see myself across a space that reminds me of the illusory palpitations which appear over macadam roads in the middle distance in midsummer heat and which, on the road ahead, creating almost credible oases, supply the driver's need for visions of water; I experience an exultant lowpitched voice sounding its echoic ululations at a caterpillar pace—how can I present it—through every hole in my upper body. In it inheres the slightly distorted quality of my own voice on tape. It is howling something, trying to hoot something, about the inconceivable Exodus.

Utterance: this it is which sets apart our labors and sentences us to tasks Medusan or liquefying, or both. What we do not calcify or make marmoreal we, like jetsam, drift in. Between shape-fixing and -shifting we suffer the projectile apprehensions of our protean attachments.

Sympathy-Meditation refers to a specific translation-process in the light of which the doer com/poses his doings, the objects; the Reception-Attribute signals a major constituent in the very shape-worker, intent on doing his do.

What is the habitus of the world which is borne over to the translator's diagnosis by the liminal ghosts of Utterance—world whose propensities he may perceive as neural, anatomical, subtle or sly? He is not quite aware of such intermittent analogical audacities; at some penultimate way-station of speculation, surrender to the delights and perils of Fascination yields to action.

Surprises inhere in the cryptic ground of the translator's thaumaturgical operations. This ground—in the context of the Path of Sympathy-Meditation—exists along with the translator's assumptions that the composition of the world is an ingathering of individual entities characterized by their

110

particulars; these are conceived of as idiosyncratically bounded, each a kind of Platonic idea of its Thingness as it were, all picked, packed and ready, set aside for perceptual collecting and labeling. Residing for the most part far below the [shuttling and prehensile elaborations of consciousness,] the translator's assumptions do not quite attain to the mettlesome certitudes of a vision of the world. The limits and anxieties of his experiences will lead him to ignore or to suppress his intuitions about the nature of the ground, which he might at best experience as agonist—constrictively or oracularly pythonic, at worst as supermarket. The Receiver is actually a Collector.

Examining the seven elements of the first of the nine *ominacunei* inscriptions, focusing upon their meanings and their interrelationships in the context of one of its possible presentations—linear and uncomplicated—we now begin to try to establish the major disjunctions in the styles of the PSM proponents and those of the PI adepts. The table of elements in the first utterance for example is simple:

How do the symbols interrelate in singular individual — as singular individual entities linearly connected to one another? • not necessarily

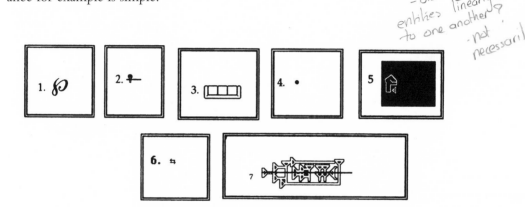

We now wander over several different courses, approaching in two more or less antithetical ways the nine *ominacunei* Seal-utterances we transcribed above. The synoptic translation was achieved by the PSM, the Path of Sympathy-Meditation, a mode effected by catalysis of translators' Reception-Attributes. The natures of both this Path and this Attribute have been distorted; they are subsumed under and often frozen by the older scholarship, receiving their names before the essential paradoxes of the categorizations had clearly manifested themselves. Now reconsideration clarifies more than efforts at renaming. "Sympathy-Meditation" and "Reception-Attribute" suggest a relationship to the world which the effective situation reverses, or at least tends to unravel. We shall see. One more time the initial utterance:

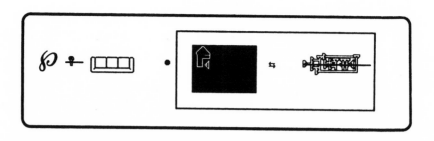

Before entering upon our double road of translation, we make brief, prefatory allusion to method number two—whose general directions our eventual carry-overs will particularize: the second method, the Path of Insertion, PI, is also known as the Path of Injection, PI: this practice is a kind of receiving attentiveness—again a widely disseminated, and vexing, character-ization which is sometimes, awkwardly, applied to the PSM as well; in contrast to the Reception-Attribute attributed to the PSM Practice, that of the PI elic-its the Filling-Attribute.

(We allow ourselves the following parenthetical observation. We will have occasion later to refer to conditions observed here, though rarely in other determinatives: the student of comparative religions will recall the five poisons, wisdoms, mantras, consorts, colors, animals, elements and orders of encompass-ing space which exist in occasionally shifting, analogous relation to the Dhyanybuddhas of Tibetan Buddhism, so for instance, as we are soon to learn, do the Seals' Entrance-Exodus Vibrations.)

The five central non-historical Asiatic energy-figures around which swirl the perfumes of such arcane soteriologies comprise—like the PI's and the PSM's—processes not beings. Are the vastnesses of linguistic operations Buddhas? This question is best appreciated by envisaging the essential How, not the what, of the Thangka-painting's practice-vectored figures. When skilfully responded to by practitioners the flux of meditational operations induces mir-rorings between Thangka and attentive devotee, kinds of mirrorings which occur also between 1. utterance and 2. translator: energy-exchanges, PSM or PI; this flux defines and heals. But in the translation practice however we see the middle term—Utterance, not merely an adjunctive mantra—which is absent in the Asian devotions to which we allude.

The table of elements is simple; but sometimes I live in the weather of my work like a gauzy pillaging ghost, which is granted or rather experiences—in a must of desire—a seizure into intermittent states of power. The ghost is egged on to yet greater efforts by the fact that the Ur-form of what it thought it had discovered turned out as often as not to embody a reflexive Medusa of the seemingly knowable. The lady leaks out of her containers as it were, and gazes at herself, the play of her hot changing eyes pointillistically seeding her world and herself with rapidly swelling masses turning rockhard. I have thought that if I could love the ground I could earn a home: nevertheless what appeared

112

Suddenly all sorts of Buddhist analogies enter in out of nowhere. - The preoccupations of the scholar.

Speaks (though rather opaquely) of his own relationship to his work,

to have been offered to quench my desire would gossamerize; alternatively it would desiccate into a landscape littered with the stones of my metamorphic assumptions. And there I was still harnessed to my desire like Ixion to his wheel in Hell, both of us having dared feed want; I think sometimes that any object of our desire bears the secret names of our incapacities, names to which our sanity forbids us access; therefore I am now advancing very carefully in the direction of the elementary.

[margin, handwritten: knowledge, understanding becomes this object but its attainment is illusory.]

So now. The path of Sympathy-Meditation marries the translator to the elements of the utterance-world preconceived as separated out into their own uniquenesses. There are fewer opacities which resist translation in the PI efforts—they direct themselves toward a world experienced as essentially unitary and which gives rise to stuffs whose boundaries are established through acts effected by the genius of the PI worker's language, or his subsuming practice. The practitioner of the Filling-Attribute is the inseparable paradox of his world.

Before we begin to examine how adepts of the Path of Sympathy-Meditation and of the Path of Insertion/Injection exercise perception and transmission, we take note of one further variable which gravely affects meaning.

Ominacunei segments are sometimes subject to Entrance-Exodus Vibration (E-E.V.): The word is *never quite the thing* nor is it ever *quite not-the-thing.* The degree and type of Vibration affecting a particular segment are codified within my diacritical pointers; the Vibration has traditionally been subsumed under the appellation of Anguish-Sign. Neither M/T/D nor U/T/I, the E-E.V. associates itself rather with the fundament of Gesture as indissolubly One with Thing: the process, forever shy of finality, runs on, endlessly increasing the rate of its movement, endlessly approaching Full Gesture. The six vibration-signs, in a helix of increasing oscillations—like the seven color-names in the Western spectrum—offer quiddities of the E-E.V. range.

[margin, handwritten: To what extent the icon is equivalent to the thing it represents [Words are at a remove from the world]]

Things will not stand still for the fix of their names; on a popular, imprecise level the signs have been taken to relate to lessening or increasing Word/Thing Separation, or SLOWS. Though coarse-grained this exoteric assumption does its part in helping to demonstrate the functions of the E-E.V.

As a matter of convenience then we conflate the Vibrations and the SLOWS. The process eventuates in three categories, each composed of two degrees.

Take, say, the icon of the third-level Torque of Separativeness,

 . Apply to it the diacritical distinctions by which I denote the activity of the E-E.V., whose presence is denoted by an overstrike (the student may find it useful to conceive of the icon as "under the erasure of the ordinary"):

The overstruck element will never manifest in its ground form; it will present in α) overstruck italics:

or in β) overstruck outline form:

or in γ) overstruck shadow form:

The overstruck forms may exist in a Transition-Phase of the second degree, signaled by an enveloping broken-lined ellipse:

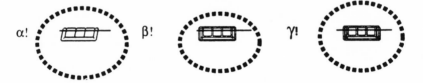

Transition-Phase α!, characterized by the least E-E.V. spin, embodies the qualities and expressive textures of ordinary speech; Transition-Phase β!, seized of medium spin, demonstrates qualities and textures of what may be envisaged as a kind of "Sprechstimme"; Transition-Phase γ!, characterized by intense spin, manifests the qualities and expressive textures of Song, that is, of Full Gesture.

An E-E.V. in both Transition-Phases may modulate either the pictographic or the cuneiform segments of an *ominacuneus.* Their anachronistic, simultaneous presences constitute an unexampled ground for speculations about the field they share. Reconstructive surgery is haunted by the middens, templates and sacks of Memory, which is Invention. The pictographs will carry to term the immanent sharp-edged Others, which in turn will bear themselves into their ultimate alphabetic closures.

The recent, first volume of the University of Pennsylvania Sumerian Dictionary contains no cuneiform script, as if transliteration into abc's serves to render original meanings. The shapes are lost. The dictionary's American morphemes indicate; but they evidence neither texture nor taste nor sight-flash of the glosses of the world incarnated in the [wedge-dances] and their ancestral archaic images—as if a singer's voice were conveyed by a phonetic transcription.

Or, rather, as if a painting were internalizable and realizable through the enumerations of its spectral particulars

or, rather, as if the [utterances of a small forest] could exhale themselves towards a ready student by a transmogrification into a detailed list of the number of the forest's trees and bushes, of the weight of its brush, of the degrees and minutes of its nests, epiphytes, worms, insects, grubs, lianas, of seeds fallen and of seeds still integral with their origin, or the mass of its canopy, of the average height of the growths comprising its climax vegetation

or, rather, as if the calculus of the vectors in the descents of its wind-afflicted, moisture-conditioned, temperature-sensitized, gravity-moderated seeds were adequate to the needs of a large inquiry.

What sorts of things store concepts?

Over hundreds of years the skin of figures in the archaic Great Sign Family sloughed off at glacial speed, mortifying evidence of terminal Toxic Epidermal Necrolysis—TENS—and progressive, ineluctable revelations of raw, sanguine dermal layers. The vessels and nerves of the Great Iconic Corium are exposed by the accreting blast of *sapiens* desires; exodus, a karmic parturition is set into motion from the great deeps of Being, expelling the infectious, highly toxic exudae of the alphabet.

Such is this burning from the inside out, directly related to pictographic thrombocytopenia. Such accelerating reduction of the pictographic platelets leads ultimately to the infestation of the moon and of the nearer planets.

The (gravid) pictograph gives birth to its successive alterations; it pupates and waits in the germplasm of its deadly potential of reconfiguring force, in its millennial eocycle of gradual swelling, to come into the rupture of the enclosing world-picture-bag married to the object-seeking eye. The pictographers by the tumid banks of Sumerian rivers draw in the anchoring present of their pictures. They are co-extensive with the Ground of secret changes. The fated pictographs—cuticle, cocoon, case—exist at the pleasure and will of the in-dwelling alphabetic larvae undergoing millennial histolysis.

The lean, ubiquitous alphabet has won—imago stage, finality, absolute presence. The wings of the alphabetic imago are constituted of its absolutely neutral transparency, anchored nowhere. What is so wonderful as the alphabet, totally available to any language in the world, pure sonic sign unstained by any local, autochthonous costume or fury, barely available to the encrustations or reshapings of history, chromosomal starfleet retained in a 2000-year gestation until time was come for the Phoenicians' poisonous gift to the world.

Thus the utterances under study engage our stern attention all the more. They require of us a threefold attentiveness. In the examination of each Seal, as well as of the sequence, we must attend to the total field of equivalents or imbalances. We must respect apparently minor variables. We may not side-step a recognition of the world-conceptions which undergrid each of the two major translation Paths. The reader will note that the following investigations engage us a bit differently from those which attended to sample utterances at the beginning of this Tablet.

I erred in calling Brad De Lisle's synoptic "song." In the course of these Laboratory-Teachings-Memoirs I increasingly recognize that most if not all translations produced under the aegis of the PSM rarely attain Full Gesture. De Lisle respects the slightly narrative thrust of the Seal sequence; he evidences juxtapositional skills. His gleanings are the seizures of a willful hierarch. He yields to misreadings due to selective inattention and ignores the driving constraints of his Path. How do these constraints manifest themselves?

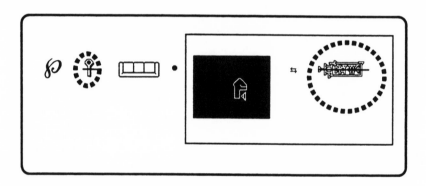

We recall the table of the elements in the first Seal. Many practitioners of the Reception-Attribute of the PSM have long implied that theirs is a sacerdotal watch-and-wait. But where is the form-arising in the picked, packed and ready sacks of the PSM multiverse? No arising, no descending; no arising or descending, no vibration; no vibration, inanition. The subtle "seizures of a willful hierarch" disclaim manipulative responsibility by simulating a particular kind of hunt. The hidden hunter waits by his trap, attends to the prey's fall and harvests his parcel of tribute. If it doesn't match the image in his desire, he waits again. He becomes his narrowing habit of power, a kind of religious.

The matter is not one of world cut-ups or no cut-ups. It is so hard to divagate upon the distinctions between the PSM and the PI, the latter term an exoteric misnomer; Insertion/Injection does present world in field-focus, but it dualistically offers it as Other. Thus it might be useful, when we meditate upon the nature of PI, to conceive of it as the Path of Assertive Mirroring-Actualization; our work may earn its merit through a recognition and acknowledgment of the seamlessness of world-tissue; we could be translated into the net of world-reflection. The PI, unlike the PSM, grants no value to self-unforgiving blasts of the desire for an exodus from the common tissue of our sentience.

First, as to the tone of De Lisle's work:

stress, pain, destroy, closed regions, cleaver, violence,
despair, terror-paces, prisoner, fistula, epilepsy, venom,
cut-off at the desire-notch, pierceable, corkscrew-hunger…

Only a determined end-run around the archaic totality of the *ominacunei* could result in the somber and inappropriate projections of his synoptic version. We will see that his "song" from a minor prophet's height accepts a world preliminarily *experienced* as pieced-out. Thus, it *is* so. In charge of the current salvage-corps, he receives staccato bundles of disparate images. He has chosen to leap over crucial diacritical alterations in utterance-elements.

Element 2,  , Body-Declension "standing," overstruck and shadowed, exists in E-E.V. Transition-Phase γ !;

Element 7,   , "exorcist," "father," outlined and

overstruck, is subject to E-E.V. Transition-Phase β !

The idiosyncratic language of the *ominacunei* shares a basic attribute with the language of the tablets we have presented in our earlier labors: it is essentially uninflected; word-order governs its organization. These are the crucial facts which underline our unflagging focus on two major aspects of this mirage-like system, seemingly so available and yet so jealous of its genial mixture of, at once, the clear edge and the allusive and evanescent. Although I consider it appropriate to use the word "mixture," I confess the word "compound" arises in my thoughts as I apprehend the uncanny aroma of totality within each Seal.

(Some contemporary poets working in language families which use alphabetic scripts—Turkish, Romanian, Tibetan, Estonian, American—might find our work useful. Present aesthetic and philosophical transvaluations may fertilize fields and point language-hands in the direction of linguistic metamorphoses. These husbandmen now serve systems unflavored by the immense allusive powers and the multiple sensations associated with logograph and ideogram.)

Now we have seen that Element 2, the Body-Declension ⚮ , "standing," attains, through its intense Entrance-Exodus Spin, γ!, to the condition of Song, Full Gesture. The expression

on the right side of Seal 1 lives in a more moderated E-E.V., *sprechstimme*, a Vibration, one might say, of the middle way between song and common speech. De Lisle ignores these diacritical interventions. Only by including them within our looking and thinking can we begin to speculate about the tiny cosmos of the Seal.

Every Seal is comprised of two roughly equal segments, arrayed on either side of a bullet, •, Element 4.

On the left side of each Seal, with the exception of Seal 5, the Broken-Scissor U/T/I of Solitary Reading and Subsuming Position Determinative,

𝄞 , introduces the utterance. In 5 the icon of the Departing Man, 🚶 , substitutes for the U/T/I in the gouged-out initial site.

Again, except for lacunae in Seals 2 and 4, also filled by the Departing Man, every Seal features a Body-Declension indicator; the one in Seal 7, represented as white on a black ground, weighs at least twice as much as the average for that particular icon.

Seals 1, 5, 6, 7, and 9 contain the first, second or third degrees of the Torque of Separativeness, Seal 5 with a puzzling repetition of second-degree Torque, which is most likely a scribal error.

In only one case, that of Seal 6, do we find an M/T/D, the Icon of Ambiguity.

The right sides of Seals 1, 2, 3, 5, 6 and 8 feature archaic pictographs in the initial position, which in Seals 4, 7 and 9 reveals rodent toothmarks. The pictographs in Seals 1, 5 and 6, white on a black ground, present as in the previously given case on the left side of Seal 7. In all Seals, save for Seal 7, the sign

/ appears in penultimate position. There again 🚶 takes the place of ꜱ .

Nothing is clearer, or more impressive, than the dynamic, the electroverbal, balance represented here. At the start of my researches I was more convinced than I am now of the degree to which these Seals comprise an exoteric rescension of Tablet IX. A more matured hypothesis awaits further examination of associated data. Although I hesitate to put the point too strongly, there is something about the construction of these nine units that suggests more than a substantive, hermeneutical striving. I cannot escape the suspicion that the architecture of the Seals reveals the ludic joy of mathematical sensation, playmind.

Having done a brief tour through the general structure of the nine *ominacunei*, we now return to our study of Seal 1, but in a clearer referential context.

We now consider rare but extremely significant variants of Elements 2, 4 and 7, to which De Lisle apparently had no access; in addition Element 5 subsumes at least three significations besides its generally recognized meaning of "eat."

First, as to the power distribution in this tiny cosmos; relevant substitutions made, we have:

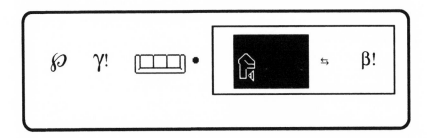

In several known instances of the icon y, "standing," the context clearly indicates the meaning to be "time."

Given the cartouche-like rectangle annealing the pictographic and cuneiform utterances on the right segment of every Seal, the bullet, •, seemed simply to separate that segment from the one on the left. But I was convinced that each Seal, though part of a sequence, had been conceived in an integral complexity. Thus the probable reductionism of the assumption about the bullet's function encouraged me to search for alternative readings. Fortunately the Staatliches Museum in Berlin made available to me a large number of uncatalogued archaic holdings, which revealed incontrovertible evidence of a very early reading for •: "water."

Recent investigation into the semantic values of the pictograph 🏠, "eat," in the right segment of Seal 1, has yielded "nose," "ear" and "finger," the first two formation by association, the latter formation by extention.

The cuneiform logogram ⌗⌗⌗ ,"exorcist," is composed of the cuneiform utterance for "father," followed by the determinative usually following fish names, infixed within the cuneiform for "mouth" (cf. the detailed

presentation of Seal 1-9 cuneiform units). We now know that ⌗⌗⌗ also bears the meanings "darkness" and "eye."

The latter term, one of the first appearances of the "antithetical meanings of primal words," exists in productive contrast with "darkness," itself a variant produced associatively, with the root "exorcist" as referent. We attempt a carryover of the root-paradigm:

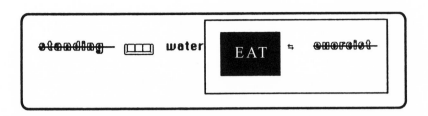

To call this procedure translation does little justice to its complexity. We might clarify its nature by adding the adjective *graphodiacritical* or by substituting for "translation" the noun *function-transfer*. This process is undeniably impoverishing; but those who come after us may consider these efforts as usable initial steps in trekking over this uncharted terrain.

We now return to an assessment of the power distribution within Seal 1. I persist in advancing very carefully in the direction of the elementary: we have already ascribed to γ!—within the context of the E-E.V.—a value of 3, and to β! a value of 2; near the beginning of our deliberations we awarded to any icon in white upon a black ground a weight double that of its associated cuneiform.

So we would have a 3, twisted by the most powerful Torque, on the left; the 2 on the right cannot be directly related to the reversed icon within the cartouche-rectangle "eat," because it does not belong to the family of the E-E.V.'s. Thus it offers no common terms with the other elements; an assessment of powers is not the same as a statement about weight.

What remains, as it does so often in such labors as these, requires intuitive responses guided by long experience. For me the decisive element in the non-equation is the powerful Torque ▢▢▢ , whose action—unlike the simpler interventions of Tablet XXVI's M/T/D Blocker ◿ , constitutes a subtle and deracinating energy. These impressions might lead the investigator to assign to the right side a higher voltage, as it were. But there is more.

We now present yet another, more inclusive, presentation of the tiny cosmos of Seal 1.

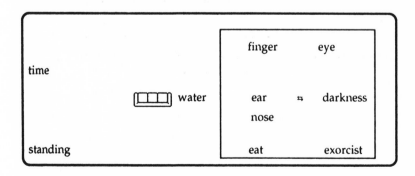

The ultimate configuration:

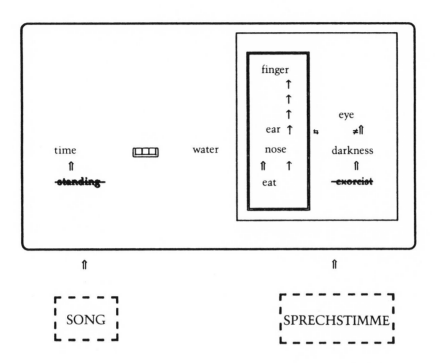

Let us say that these roots and ejaculate energies partake of three very old confluences: language-water, language-time, language-darkness. We approach this body by means of the PI. Here I must repeat an earlier comment:

> Thus it might be useful, when we meditate upon the nature of the PI, to conceive of it as the Path of Assertive Mirroring-Actualization; thereby our work may earn its merit through a recognition and acknowledgment of the seamlessness of world-tissue, and we could ourselves be translated into the net of world-reflection. The PI, unlike the PSM, grants no value to the self-unforgiving blasts of the desire for an exodus from the common tissue of sentience.

. . . or that these ejaculate rotations
blind cave-shrimp in a glaucous under-river arrive
into floods of exploring
    no lintel sill jamb frame,
               why

does a genius of place always carry you off from your house
if not that you show yourself
ready the fields the tremulous fields of action, wounds, the dark glow
of the barely possible, anarchic
                                  ... let's say arrive through the blind
artificer's ferreting hands to the corrugated
soil or the worm-rich lapsus-loam there are fingers
treating of ridges treating there they palpate fractures premature
calcifications the dawn light's cries of the rough edges
of designing vocables and who   sees?
                                    eye   from an eye
the seeking rainbow-cords link to the object, not-two, it's the sentence of the
eater
sitting in the court of surprise

... or that this tongue
arrive for the sour and sweet macerated word-mash
cave-shrimp blind taste crust of the common
denotation

~~quiet, pantherly, open to predawn susurrations, the Old Ones~~
~~drawn by a wake, the exodus of the curved...~~   ~~happy~~
~~for the modern, they overhear at the edge of their murmur~~
~~the gorgeous coming powers~~
~~choice~~

        the eye!   the cadence of the eye!
     the sought, seduced appropriating traveler in the two
of one place, seduceable through an apparent end of separation
               ... the voices!
                    look, see them in the azury center
falling—
             ... or that the nostrils be guiltless of seeking
                                    meditating
nostrils no flare of nostrils   scow-stink hyacinthine odors
of utterance-shards
                 ... or that through hammer stirrups anvil in a surface-rising
edged and common sound-bond a transfer is being taken on
                              identity say a
boom
a tweet a magna-decibelled-shudder receiving an osseous tremble

~~opened the Old Ones drawn by exodus~~

so this world is the one
it constitutes our food language-food we eat and we are
translatable let's say equidistant from every point or we are
a bloody loin of soul like them that's all right language-cannibal bait

~~...building and dreamed 4 into the joy~~

~~placelessness~~

TABLETS JOURNALS / DIVAGATIONS

A collection of quotations taken from sources ranging from Jung to Chogyam Trungpa + his own notes / reflections.

Some of this is explicit commentary on the poem itself (topics, themes, methods, characterizations) + some remarks on poetry in general. Highlight certain aspects, make manifest his intentions

  - a real treat after struggling through the opaqueness of the poem itself + also to have such an upfront honest rendering of his poetic - really he's exposing himself in a way, opening his arms to the reader, welcoming us into his world

Brings up a lot of really pertinant issues surrounding poetry in our times

A Tablet?: chant of nonsense syllables, transliterated. The Tablet people liked "nonsense." But we people try to turn everything into sens

A Tablet?: layers like the J and H etc. variant sources of the O.T. books thru *Joshua*.

A Tablet?: The verb is *time-past* etc. and *conceptual*. Its absence to add to nominal immediacy.

A Tablet: The Rorschach idea

The Tablet of Shapes

The Tablet of the child's power to change himself into whatever

One Tablet completely [   ]!

The Tablets: Animism: who is walking? what is it in the self that talks? is there a self-envelope for what talks?

The Tablet of Peripheries

The Tablet of Dissidence (Lautréamont?)

The Tablet of the Great Dissidence

what is 'I'?

In the Tablets, how does one individual man come across? how's his psyche/context?
      like "is the man a bird"
         "is the man four-legged and with teeth"
         "is the man a tree"

a berdache Tablet

man in the beginnings of his being forked in 2 on the 2-halved Tablet: but not sure the parts are correctly put together.

Animals Tablet: translation troubles

The Tablets: formal games and invention give rise to substantive concerns *and* social reality.

127

The scholar-translator himself has different moods, heightenings

really fantastic: the sequence from hieroglyph, cuneiform, syllabary, alphabet ....
relativity of all things to the imaginative makings. Zones. Texts of the "future"
—"Science-fiction" of the past confounding temporality. Who is speaking?

Psychological freedom for me for lewdness, bawdy, irony, satire, unplumbable
misery = *tones*

think lots about what the Vision is

The Tablets: Weird sense of distance—and closeness—"alienation effect"?—
(avoid weaknesses of *Marat/Sade*.)

Why leave fictive experiments to the prose writers?

arrangements? intercalations? order?

A Tablet: Palimpsest w/transparent paper?

asthma Tablet

A Tablet: "la représentation de l'espace chez l'enfant." (Piaget)

A Tablet: "le dévelopment de la notion de temps, de mouvement, vitesse..."

A Tablet: "genèse de l'idée du hazard..."

The commentator takes on a more active part. His "notes" become "poems."
What does that mean? What are the differences in the first place? "Poem" is
what?

A Tablet like the bird that flies up its own asshole? Möbius analogue?

motion
        &
            monumentality
            (as *Ivan the Terrible*)

homo ludens   *Playing w/ the idea of homo ludens. Many different levels of joking: w/in the tablets, in the construct surrounding our confrontation w/ them.*

"the consanguinity of all forms of life seems to be a general presupposition of
mythical thought."

                                        —Cassirer

All life forms interrelated

occasionally, places from which suddenly energy comes .... mottos to wake, cut through the accumulated trivia of repetition. "Le vent se lève; il faut tenter de vivre..." Also the high resonance of repetition.

I'm mortally affected by others' <u>categories;</u> they damp up my ease; they are *a prioris.* Fuck them. They constitute Authority.

[handwritten: Breaking w/ traditional literary catagories. Combining poetry, scholarship, memoir etc. as a willful act of defiance]

withdrawal and return

<u>who is talking</u>?

Yeats says poetry to be "ascetic, ecstatic, austere."

the silence of a Reverdy poem

Indian thought: the absence of Time. How do you do that if you're also <u>playing History</u>?

Anxiety is the angel. Open it all up.

<u>is man the only animal that laughs?</u> *[handwritten: humour]*

<u>a good comedian is not a successful mystic. Is this true</u>? The necessary spontaneity of the good comedian makes him yield to the world of the audience. The conflict between the comedian and the mystic can make poems.

the greatest daring is in resisting what comes easily.

"You would find it ridiculous if, when you asked someone his name, he replied, 'My name is whatever you like to call it.' You would find such an answer ridiculous. And if he were to add, '<u>I have whatever name you care to give me, and it is my real name,</u>' you would consider him mad. And yet that is what we must perhaps get accustomed to: indeterminacy become a positive fact, a positive element of knowledge."

—Valéry

verbal art for our time, since Rimbaud anyhow, has grazed the refusals of both the word and the world. Silence and isolation.... Irony is one weapon in the refusal of complicity for the world's tawdriness, will's abdication another. <u>Poetry is the processual impulsion toward identity, an identity which is intermittently arrived at through image and through pattern.</u> Each poem is a new start from a minutely different place.

experience not "feeling" makes it new.

129

lack of a point of view—i.e. who's speaking? and to whom?

poem: cubism/rotating viewpoint and the noumenal form of the childhood of man. (?)

the pernicious aspects of "performance"; the quest for "failure."

not poetry as obeisance to the sacred, but as a creation of it in all its activity; not as an appeal for its survival in spite of a corrosive sense that the sacred is lost. but as a movement which itself might add its own small measure to reality.

why stop at human speech, remembering the "consanguinity of all forms of life"? If categories disappear and if genres disappear, if it is the new perspective which shows the essence of what had been cliché or unseen, if the Gnostics have meaning (if they *are*) we cannot have a Babel of tongues if they are the speech of the poem. Joyce started it. Extension of the dramatic monologue into plurilogue.

the rhythmic and melodic interval alterations, variations in Hindu, linear, non-harmonic music suggest the richness of the medium in which they live.

"There is something amazing about the survival of metaphysical endeavor. Though under constant attack, from the religious..., the artists..., of the scientist and the positivist philosopher, it continues to survive. Apparently no person of intelligence is exclusively religious, artistic or scientific ... there is in metaphysics a challenging search for reality which remains significant despite error and incompleteness."

—Ulick

since metaphysics is not art, the artifact must exist in time, and be partial, and be—to however small a degree—"constructed." Is this sad?

Coomaraswami: "Primitive man, despite the presence of his struggle for existence, knew nothing of merely functional arts. The whole man is naturally a metaphysician, and only later on a philosopher and psychologist, a systematist. His reasoning is by analogy, or in other words by means of an 'adequate symbolism.' As a person rather than an animal he knows immortal through mortal things." Is it important that this be true? If it *is* important, is it true?

the poet is a namer.

there is no nuclear self.

130

there is no nuclear self.

The made thing, poem, artifact, product, will appear to the maker as Other and yet give the pleasure of recognition, to breed other discoveries. The voices in the made thing, poem, object, need no ascription by the maker. He does not know the necessary identity of a voice or many voices. They speak him in a way he later discovers. The locus appears later.

The joy of tachisme, play.... freedom in the concrete small materia poetica....

"In the highest circle an ultimate mystery stands behind the polyvalence of pictorial forms, and the flickering light of the intellect is snuffed out."

—Klee

poetry of the insane.

Poetry must make us live and perceive more intensely, not by the direct use of symbols, but by a religious concern for the present real—the destruction of almost dead categories and nostalgia. Only from such destructions will present life arise. Urban destructions.

"In all perception we have to do only with variable alterations that have a particular structure; these various time-structures we experience qualitatively through various concepts. A repetition has the smallest degree of alteration, a wholly surprising event the greatest ....The degree of information is thus greatest when at every moment of a musical flow the momentum of surprise is greatest: the music constantly has 'something to say.' But this means that the experiential time is in a state of flux, constantly and unexpectedly altering .... If we realize, at the end of a piece of music that we have 'lost all sense of time,' then we have in fact been experiencing time most strongly." *and with a book too?*

—Stockhausen: *Structure and Experiential Time*

The aim of my poetry is to reduce the "gulf between the unconscious and the ego." *— why quotes?*

Starve the desire for fact and empiricism when your personality needs it and you enslave as well the imagination.

"To the extent that I managed to translate the emotions into images—that is to say, to find the images which were concealed in the emotions—I was inwardly calmed and reassured. Had I left those images hidden in the emotions, I might have been torn to pieces by them. There is a chance that I might have succeeded in splitting them off; but in that case I would inexorably have fallen into a neurosis and so been ultimately destroyed by them anyhow."

—Jung: *Memories, Dreams, Reflections*

(In that sense, and one that gives the poet the privilege of registering the quakes rather than insisting upon them, the mode of the dramatic characterizes much of poetry. Poetry as that playful and difficult activity which is a part of the life-effort to heal the self....the disparate and disjunctive modes and voices of *The Tablets* occur as they occur, proliferating one-ly.)

"The artist might well ask how, in such a spinning world as ours, he is to know that he stands in the *present* .... there are clues. Since he must live and have his being in a world of clichés, he will know this new world by their absence. He will know it by the fact that he has not been there before. The true territory ahead is what he must imagine for himself. He will recognize it by its strangeness...."

—Wright Morris: The Living Novel

In confession everything matters; the main effort of the confess-er is telling how he feels; in art selection operates, from the nature of the imagination, *the maker of* concepts. The main pleasure in what's called art probably comes from the conceivable possibility of some transitory order.

Good taste is boredom and death.

"Singer's stories reverberate with the most awesome possibilities; and so they appear to reflect more astutely the dominant pessimisms of our age. Setting his tales of demons turned into men and men becoming demons in .... exotic graveyards within the extinct landscape of the Yiddish speaking Jews, Singer has so imbued his cast of talmudists, peasants and housewives with obsessively modern passions that the works take on a vivid uncanniness as if some of our own obsessions were reflected therein .... the use of the supernatural is a spiritual shorthand for the world."

—Ellman in the NY Times Book Review, May 1966

also; Poetry is the product of Joy

Prose is eloquence, wants to instruct, to convince; wants to produce in the soul of the reader a state of knowledge. Poetry is the producer of joy, its reader participates in the creative act. Thus Commentary and Text in *The Tablets*? (Is that distinction stupid?) ___ *No but maybe inappropriate*

Shakespeare: Lear/simplicity to complex self-awareness to madness to rebirth to death
Swift: Gulliver/simplicity to complex observations to madness to madness
Schwerner: Pinitou?
            Scholar-Translator?
(you arrogant freak ...

"You can interpret that painting in 10 different ways [Bosch: *Garden of Delights*]. You can interpret it from an alchemist's point of view, a philosophical point of view, a Catholic point of view, a Freudian point of view, an aesthetic point of view—it's endless. Life's like that too. Everybody's right."

—Jean-Jacques Lebel, *Boss*, Spring 1967

"For at least I know, with certainty, that a man's work is nothing but the long journeying to recover, through the detours of art, the two or three simple and great images which first gained access to his heart. And that is perhaps why, at forty, after twenty years of work and publication, I continue to live with the notion that my work is not begun."

—Camus: preface to 1975 ed. of *L'Envers et L'Endroit*

And suppose the fear of any discovered world is so great as to make writing almost impossible?

The blurring between fixes: attention must be paid. That is, to the necessary, unavailable, tenses between the few tenses that we have in English, those that tempt us into believing that grammatical orders of reality have anything to do with our experience. That is, to the child's good sense in the art appreciation classroom between slide and slide. He is told that slide *a*—Titian—is a finished painting because it is a finished painting and that a micron could be added or changed only at the risk of destroying the whole; he is told the face in slide *b*—Van Gogh—incorporates weariness-decayed hope-internalized conflict-transpersonal love. He learns never to ask How do you really know when *a*, or anything, is finished? He knows never to say The face on *b* makes me happy and seems to me happy. It's all a plot to make him accept a nuclear self. There is none, and his whole life will depend on that discovery. Then the discontinuity of time and consciousness will destroy him, or it will not. If it does not, his happiness springs from another discovery: intermittent epiphanies make the discontinuity bearable; the fixes take on their appropriate embodiment of the ridiculous and he moves like a dance within the germplasm of the blurrings. Any willfull overorchestration of poetry removes that existential element of the gratuitous. The Space inside the poem is the necessary precondition for a perception of infinity. *The Tablets* live in a matrix of unbreachable, ambiguous and antique silence; irony: the Old Ones had a futurity and we've deep down almost lost the sense of one. *The Tablets* also exist within a context of Heisenbergian invention. Are *The Tablets* then blurrings within those two fixes, one unbreachable, the other scientifically "up-to-date"?

[handwritten marginal note: b/c we've given up on it, admitted defeat?]

Except it's the particular order of Babel the particular poet chooses. The poet has not liberated himself from demons. The rationalist has done that. The poet has successfully exercised a series of potentially fruitful choices; he ends up with the pursuing demon that his death-mask will resemble if his life has been a success.

133

Why he chose this format

The modern, accidental form of Sumero-Akkadian tablets provides me with a usable poetic structure. They offer, among other things, ways out of closures—which I find increasingly onerous—as well as the expansion of the syntactical girdle of English. They also invite spontaneous phonetic improvisations. The uses of the past, by means of these found archaic objects, are thus more than ironic and other than nostalgic. The context of sober translation creates a mode suitable for seductions by the disordered large which is the contemporary, and the narrative, which is out of honor in the most relevant modern poetry. The context also makes me feel comfortable in recreating the animistic, for which I have great sympathy, and which, subject to my sense of the present, I have not been able to approach as poet without such contextual personae and forms as I have found in these archaic leftovers.

More specifically, I'm excited by being able to put in holes wherever I want, or wherever they need to be; on the other hand I can fill out some of the infinite interstices which exist—unavailable segments of the continuum—between the pathetically restricted categories of English tenses; in addition, I'm interested in what happens to a modern concept of personality and its sense of non-vegetative duration when that self, say me, makes certain antique allowances.

Eliot and Pound structured ironic and tragic commentaries by confronting past and present. Why not go further, I thought, and recreate the past itself, in a series of subjectively ordered variations suggestively rooted in the archaic? And, more, why not augment the confusions between illusion and reality by the further invention of a scholar-translator whose fictive but oppressively present self would add a dimension of narration? This might be one way in which the "what happened next" could be restored to functional poetic usefulness in an age of what Simone Weil called "decreation." The holes in the text and the dubious provenances then act as counterweights to the squareness of conventional linear narrative continuity. The personality of the narrator himself gradually reveals its own idiosyncratic variables: even within the fictive frame of *The Tablets*, can he be trusted? The problems of "translations"... To what degree is any poem a translation, or a thereness?

What is more, the rapid shifts in tonality and texture found in some archaic and primitive materials contribute a helpful antidote to "civilized" modes concerned with characterological and dramatic imperatives of consistency. Contemporary media mixes, for instance, are another—if often mechanical—manifestation of the revolutionary impulse pushing against classical *and* romantic canons. In addition, the tonal and textural shifts, the comic vision of these *Tablets* (can a man talk about his own vision and not laugh?) help to place in some perspective the contemporary mystique of line-endings and their poetic importance. The question is not Where does the line end; the question is What is meaningfulness? The final question is When are a man's discoveries techniques subsumed in his vision; and When are his inventions gimmicks straining to support a petty order of limits?

Poetry, as game, as act of faith, as celebration, as commemoration, as epic praise, as lyric plaint, as delight in pattern and repetition—poetry is in trouble. Not any more trouble than the Earth, concepts of nobility and self-lessness, senses of utility, hope. But that's not saying too much. Whoever most largely perceives decreation may find himself praising entropy in self-defense. Or, if he is a poet, constitutionally unable to go all the way to formlessness and the joy of envisioning the running down of systems, he looks around for a way to make lasting monuments out of vaseline and lacunae.

> Loss of a sense of satisfying personal identity is linked to mod-
> ern man's inevitable loss of the "games" learned early in life.
> In other words, modern man, if he is at all educated, cannot
> play the same sorts of games which he played as a youngster,
> or which his parents played, and remain satisfied with them.
> Cultural conditions are changing so rapidly that everyone
> tends to share the problem of the immigrant who *must* change
> games because he has moved from one country to another.
> Even those who stay put geographically find themselves in a
> world other than that of their parents. Indeed, as they grow
> older they usually find themselves in a world other than that
> of their youth. In this dilemma, man is confronted by the
> imperative need to relinquish old games and to learn to play
> new ones. Failing this, he is forced to play new games by old
> rules, the old games being the only ones he knows how to
> play. *This fundamental game-conflict leads to various problems in liv-*
> *ing* .... A type of game-conflict develops from the realization
> that man can play no transcendentally valid (God-given)
> game. Many react to this insight with the feeling that, in this
> case, *no game is worth playing.* The significance of this condi-
> tion—namely that *no game is really worth playing*—appears to
> be especially great for contemporary Western man.
> —Thomas Szasz, *The Myth of Mental Illness*

"...*mouvement*," says Marcel Raymond, talking, among others, about Valéry, "*de retrait et d'exhaustion qui s'observe chez plus d'un contemporain.*" A con-dition, nevertheless, through which the poet and his friends theorize about the Good Place.

A fish can only swim. If a poem is a fish it must discover that swim-ming's what it does. Sympathy. Sympathy. But how about that ocean, the world, where it gets harder and harder to set up categories of the real and unre-al as tenable hypotheses? The immense difficulty of defining a self, of assum-ing an identity, goes along with this. In poetry then silences and lacunae should *be*—and being, act—and the often arbitrary distinctions between concrete and abstract, real and unreal, sane and mad, objective and subjective seem increas-

135

[margin note, top left, handwritten:] The incroachments modern life has on our minds + our poetries.

ingly irrelevant. To demonstrate the arbitrariness by the processual flux of the poem .... Destroy the point of view: who's speaking? to whom? and the rest of it.

The medieval realities. Unverbalized assumptions even *now* more real than we would believe. God the Father, goodness, the fixed beautiful Chain of Being, the *Spiritual Exercises*, as real as skywriting. (When we see the past as poetic horde of instructions, we overlook the ghetto, the Inquisition, the *auto-da-fé*, the plagues ....) The ladders and links of that gone world play through *Macbeth*; the world there gone awry, the fevers of the body, distempers in the Kingdom, the shaking state of man: for Shakespeare the meanings of a broken world move him to consider the fixed regime and ordered state disturbed. Macbeth does not despair at his wife's death: he fights the enemy. Macduff immediately shifts from agony over his wife's and children's murders to resolute defiance of Macbeth. The "real" world is always available, always stands as recourse, a stage for redressive action; and Fortinbras always restores health to the rotten disjointed time: Hamlet and Macbeth are next-door neighbors. The Post-Medieval Age, even, is gone and its "wholeness," now perceivable, its faith in rationality and technology and science—available now through the same mythical tense as the hierarchy of angels—had presented the only order we share.

There was an outside in that place of order, a place to go *from* which to look at madness, at the destroyed land/water/air. Nothing matters more than the realization that there are no places left *from which* to look at madness, at the destroyed land/water/air; we must accept the only possibilities available; there is no nuclear self; there is no *unendurable* inward or outward Babel of tongues, there is merely Babel; we must admit dooming simplicism that inheres in prestructured categories. To alter structure? And how radically? In what direction? How does the poem live?

How will the mind work? By the eidetic confrontation of the "real"? The real changes. By feeling through Cassirer's moving elaboration of the primitive ethos as "the consanguinity of all living things"? Intermittently at best, and with the edge of despair for being so irrevocably far. The real changes. The uncertainty principle in art, a function of interchange between phenomena and poet .... The aim: to discover in the self as many different cat- *[margin mark: ⁾]*
[margin mark, handwritten: ✳/] egories of perception as possible. The made thing, poem, artifact, product, will appear to the maker as Other and yet give the pleasure of recognition, to breed other discoveries. The voices: the maker does not know the identity of a voice or many voices. They speak to him in a way he later discovers. The locus appears later.

But the enemy surrounds us. Words lose their substance, are coopted by mimetic IBM ads, depress; the attitude of distrust toward words spreads to objects. We need a new language, one that we cannot speak, may not be able to speak, unseizable, proliferating like the elementary particles in physics: no end to it: uncertain statistical places left from which to look at the negative-

[margin note, bottom left, handwritten:] Advertising (+ propaganda) lead us to distrust words. Language as the medium of coersion, manipulation

136

muons which are told by their uncertain traces. The ambiguous, ambivalent?, nature of the love, need?, for schizophrenic language, pre-Christian rites, the rhythmed products of children. The aim is to get in touch but the object fades. The good society. Poetry is a body invested with rhythmic cells; it is neither the Way nor the object; its appearance makes no difference, but at least it permits the freedom to discover apparently new games. Though one tires of chance itself, and cooks a nice piece of fried zucchini. This or that: hints; the almost conceivable possibility of some transitory order. The Babel Poems.

Note on Tablet XXIV

The initial stage of *Tablet XXIV* consisted of a few widely separated sequences set down in a roughly balanced spatial configuration:

no wisdom no ice no mountains no segment
the snow and the white heron

silver bowl bright moon light

form of wind

emptiness of plant

Several months elapsed before the next phase, which involved only the addition of:

the ruminant anxiety that the old question
is the new question

inserted, without leaving extra line spaces, under and flush with "the snow......"

Tablets XX through *XXIII* seem to be a sequence of letters; they imply some continuity of person and appear to trace the decline and end of a relationship. Given the largely linear development of the narrative—though shadowed by ambiguity and overtone—I felt that *XXIV* should be a consistently self-undoing voidness. The first line—suggested, I realized later, by the *Heart Sutra*—set the essential direction.

The (unidentifiable) voices of former *Tablets*, speaking through loss, celebration, primordial need for mensuration references, grief, ecstatic sexuality, psychotic and aphasic confusion, magical incantation, formal insult-modes, parental anxiety, lover's despair...., are now joined by the unsettled music of the voice alive in the sky-veins, the ores and the brilliant ground, profoundly at home in the bright unanchoring everywhere which is equally "the darkness every time for the first time," repeated nullifications of potentially separating concepts, process in which abstract and concrete share each other's attributes.

The syncretic ground of the *Tablets*, since the mid 60s, the animistic, polytheistic and Buddhist matrices in the Tablets—the last most evidently informing *XXIV*—owe much to the needs and available choices in my own story, little to a predetermined paradigm. (The archaic pre-Christian antinomies of *kenosis* and *plerosis*, emptying and filling, characteristic of early Middle Eastern civilizations, served largely as a generalized and suggestive context.) My barely conscious but pronounced anxieties about my fatherhood informed some of the early, largely "animistic," Tablets; my increasing involvement in Tibetan, now Zen, Buddhist practice is present texture: interdependence, web of particulars, non-separation, transformation, emptiness. Since my understanding as it relates to these abstractions keeps changing from present to present, each poem is merely manifestation of, or rather, *is* "continuous practice," which as Dogen Zenji says, "is delight by virtue of the power of continuous practice."

·　　·　　·　　·　　·

"...light
From a persistent fire twitching
Reflections of our momentary flames.
My poetics has old ochre in it
On walls of a civilized cave."

—Louis Zukofsky, "A"-12

all concepts are misconceptions

Is it possible to live without a zone of comfort, of solidity?

Hélène Cixous says, "Writing is learning to die. It's learning not to be afraid, in other words to live at the extremity of life, which is what the dead, death, give us. (*Three Steps on the Ladder of Writing*, 10)

George Oppen, tell me, if there's no object constancy, what is the shipwreck of the singular? And how is it that a place to start from implies at the very least a potentially identifiable and receiving thereness...

I see now. The scholar/translator seems increasingly inclined to express aspects of his morphemalgia; it catches up with him; in *Tablet XI* following the lines "she opened her ++++++++++++++++++++++++++ and never minded/ she took him splayed from them to cover it," he says, "singular confusion of pronouns here. I do not know who I am when I read this. How magnificent." By the time he gets to *Tablet XXVII*, having so variously applied his will to the reduction of space between himself and his images, as if in prayerful appeals to his unreachable monotheistic god, he unwittingly backs into the will's splintering Other. Language-pain:

"My table of elements is simple," he says, "but sometimes I live in the weather of my work like a gauzy pillaging ghost, which is granted ... a seizure into intermittent states of power. The ghost is egged on to yet greater efforts by the fact that the Ur-form of what it thought it had discovered turned out as often as not to embody a reflexive Medusa of the seemingly knowable. The lady leaks out of her containers as it were..."

Medusa. Classicism. Humanism. The Scholar/Translator's own filters .... Let's have a look at the Scholar/Translator as partly a creature of post-Renaissance humanism and counter-reformation. This is no more arbitrary than accepting Plato as some fountain-head and Descartes as some modern philosophy ancestor, and assuming willy-nilly acceptances and rejections, but presence. Montaigne/Pascal. Bonhommie and Entrechat, with the death presence. Why am I thinking of super-subtle Pascal, his raw foundation terror of infinite

[handwritten margin note:] But his studies are of a primal animistic world —a tension b/t these 2 modes of understanding ourselves + our surroundings

139

spaces, when I consider the mindscapes of inhabitants of so many *Tablets*? inscape that is. All the anonymous voices in *Tablets* in some relationship to Montaigne in other terms? Montaigne as friend of the court of the Scholar/Translator; commonalty of Emptiness...

the air of Performance-α at Liancourt

for Michael Heller at the Muses' Tomb

No one deserves to be praised for goodness,
unless he has the potential for wickedness: any
other kind of goodness is most often only an
instance of laziness or a powerlessness of the will.

The Duc de la Rochefoucauld, *Maximes*, CCXVII

What is common in the evocations of ritual
escapes naming, and is present; what perpetuates
and intensifies division, on the other hand, exists
as an armada of names, and doesn't heal.
The poet is a namer and what he names is the most
subtilized ether, empyrean invented to fill
non-existent spaces; he lives within
the residual perfume of names, haunted
home.
            What is the nature of the recurrent hope
for the seizure of the irreducible?
We can only call it delusion if we are sure
it doesn't exist and we're not sure it does
not exist. It might be good
to name what the hope believes itself
to be pointing at. That is, it might be useful
to call the pointed-at, let's say, "Performance-α."
That embodies a claim for the radiating primacy
of the invisible. It's not the kindness
of cowards, which picks and skins
and incises and packs
a thought
and sends it along. "It is as though the Aurignacian painter
were ashamed," says Zbigniew Herbert, "of his body,
and longing for his forsaken animal family."

naming engenders separation — hmm —

140

                    Did the Duc de la Rochefoucauld in 1662
entertain in the rooms of his private
story the conceit that the four gesturers—
goodness, wickedness, laziness
and powerlessness of the will—danced subtilizing
dances which were real because the four dancers
were real? or did the Duc de la Rochefoucauld
wearied in the most private and hidden
of his private room—hard by the sweet congeries
of imported horn, polished bone, glinting shell—
was he struck by a blow at Liancourt, a blow cold
with the power of the outside air become solid
imploding inside the margins between himself
and his elaborations of the fields
of his reading? He'd reread his CCXVIIème Réflexion Morale
and imagined a moment which neighbored
the cold horizon line beyond his county's
rhetorizing limits. His nod releases
a dear companion satyr, freed
from indenture for one synaptic
quaver—
                doppleganger, through whose horned flair
the Duc de la Rochefoucauld agape smiles
that his CCXVIIème Réflexion Morale is not about anything

The spiritual inscape of *Tablets* is terror; sometimes it isn't.

Rodin: to become a confidant of the natural world....

... capturing or finding one moment after another in which the security and
pleasure of associative combination peel off, centerless: thought while attend-
ing a poetry reading of Leslie Scalapino

Student: I'm feeling spacious now
Teacher: Do you hear my heart beat?
Student: Hunh. You're too far.
Teacher: No I'm not
Student: I'll work on it.

I conceived of a grammar facilitating the arrival *into* a word through some con-
duit, to abolish Option by inhabiting utterance, prefacing utterances in the
Tablets' ur-language with various Body-Declensions—"CROUCHED-
DYING," say, or "LYING-DOWN-SICK"—to experience the utterance's
density partly through a self-cleansing into a newly considered way *in*. The

Indian artist shrives himself, does special ablutions etc. to prepare himself for the coming doing. The Body-Declensions a kind of speed-up of this process, made a very part of the utterance world.

XXVI/XXVII: To provide a context within which image might be able to attain mantric presence.

The words perceive you, in their variousness.

On the scalpel's very edge, talk!

Attend to the kilos and grams of various utterances; how represent such aspects in a writing system?

In connection with *Tablets*—It isn't my business to ratiocinate, or to vaticinate; so I do; I am then an accomplice in probable re-ratiocinations by et al. *The Tablets* incarnate a new genre: "all that's left is pattern (shoes?)," the initial line followed by song after song of demurrer and semi-presence, pick-up and drop-away of insult-poem, dirge, evocative sexualized ritual apostrophe and lesbian devotional susurrations, conflation of a cuneiformoid epistolary with a radical sense of the unsettledness of the temple language, continued slide away of referents. Here the genre of the archaeological's undone by the sense that whatever could be findable will not be findable—the meaning of the digs progressively wafting into common air—not without appearances of the epic, the psychodramatic, the irredeemable word-pain. The self-undoing genre crowded with doing.

"The mind is not regarded an internal picturing mechanism which represents the individual objects in the world, but as a faculty that discriminates the boundaries of the substances or stuffs referred to by names. This 'cutting up things' view contrasts strongly with the traditional Platonic philosophical picture of objects which are understood as individuals or particulars which instantiate or 'have' properties (universals.)"
—Chad Hansen, *Language and Logic in Ancient China.* Ann Arbor: U. of Mich. Press, 1983. [quoted in A.C. Graham, *Disputers of the Tao: Philosophical Argument in ancient China.* Lasalle IL: Open Court Press, 1989.]

"In a well-known *koan* a monk asked Master Juketsu: 'Speech spoils the transcendence of Reality, while silence spoils the manifestation. How could one combine speech and silence without spoiling Reality?' The master replied 'I always remember the spring scenery I once saw in Konan. Partridges were chirping there among fragrant flowers in full bloom.'"

"Whether we speak or remain silent, the ultimate reality in its suchness can never be indicated. For if we use language in trying to re-present the reality, the latter will necessarily become articulated on the spot, and consequently only the phenomena will be apparent and the *urgrund* while if we keep silent, the non-articulated may very well be symbolically presented, but the aspect of articulation will be left in the dark."

from "Language and Articulation," in *Toward a Philosophy of Zen Buddhism* by Lou Mitsunen Norstrom.

Words whirl, hesitate, change, are still, move in transit phases, whirl still. ...a field generating the Scholar/Translator along with the presented materiality, transformable materiality, of the word, the part-word, the utterance. The S/T proffers no information about the provenance of these forms and their variants, or about the original clay-incising methods and presentations used by the Old Ones:

Elementary particles. Energy ⇆ Mass. Or, let's say, E-E.V ⇆ Morphemes. Insistence on the word's thereness, evanescent thereness. Or, let's say, Entrance/Exodus. In from where? Coming out of what . The field is the situation. The E-E.V. wd. be the relevant *conceit*:

3a. a fanciful poetic image, especially an elaborate or exaggerated comparison
b. a poem or passage consisting of such an image
4a. the result of intellectual activity; a thought or an opinion. b. a fanciful thought or idea
5a. a fancy article; a knickknack. b. an extravagant, fanciful and elaborate construction or structure.

Let's assume each word is characterized by a certain spin. Think electron. Think Entrance-Exodus Vibration. The E-E.V spin of ordinary conversation, the medium spin a kind of *Sprechstimme*, the intensest spin Song, say, or complete Gesture. How will the S/T incorporate these figures?

Explaining the reasoning behind the E-E.V spin (sort of)

"The word is never quite the thing, nor is it ever quite not-the-thing," says the Scholar/Translator in *XXVII*. He must demonstrate some sense of his passion for—what is it—signage, linkage, it's crucial to him that he give the reader some token of immanence experienceable through the oscillating body of the phoneme, the morpheme. Everything spins. **E**ntrance-**E**xodus **V**ibration. He says: The Vibration has traditionally been subsumed under the appellation Anguish-Sign. Once again the fundamental woe of separativeness. Neither Mind/Texture Determinative nor Utterance Texture/Indicator, the E-E.V. associates itself rather with the fundament of Gesture as indissolubly One with Thing: the process, forever shy of finality, runs on, endlessly increasing the rate of its movement, endlessly approaching Full gesture..." Yes, Paul Valéry's anguish

143

in the *Cimetière Marin* over the never-quite-arriving arrow of Xeno of Elea. Oppen and the pain of materiality. Enough suffering to go around. Stevens's opening to the pain-game: "To be released," from "planetary pass-pass." To be released. We *are* the Old Ones.

"Even though the acceptance of what is happening may be confusing, just accept the given situation and do not try to make it into something else; do not try to make it into an educational process at all. Just see it, perceive it and then abandon it. If you experience something and then disown that experience, you provide a space between that knowledge and yourself which permits it simply to take its course. Disowning is like the yeast in the fermentation process. That process brews a state of mind in which you begin to learn and feel properly."
    —Chogyam Trungpa, *Glimpses of Abhidarma*. Boulder: Prajna. p. 83

★It is in that state, space of mind, that composing becomes itself,★
Poetry.

Dialogue with categories: What do I *like* to do ? do without putting off, need for validation? Read *The Times*, play tennis, make love, drive, eat .... What do I dislike? Writing, doing practice, grading papers, working with my worsening eyes, doing the business of poetry, performance and publishing. What's the comfortable, secure ambiance within which I worked successfully when I first conceived of and worked on *The Tablets* ? How do you compose a poem without calculating its potential effects? What's the pleasure, the sensation of important ongoingness, which permeated my productive life? And what changed it? I had to face and destroy the tendency towards sourness. Such destructions constitute the poetry of slogging through the trench warfare of *being entitled, insisting on what's due,* poison gas. I think of *tachisme,* starting with no root, no memory. Every pursued act has to do with the sensation of power. *Tablets* had to do with my ineluctable sense of their criminal importance, the power of my daring to embody the apparently dark and dangerous in the epic and lyrical narrative, all entropic, of the anonymous singers, clay-fraught.

For whom, towards whom, did Yeats write his *Autobiography*?

There's a negative force within me that wants to stop writing this, to go else-where, to leave as in every sesshin I've ever suffered through, almost every group I've ever involved myself with. I could now initiate analytical specula-tion about all this; it's my habit, a poor habit surely. Pleasure and power and sensation are the essential validators. The work on *The Tablets* was not the result of a "divine madness"; it involved clear thinking in radiant context of self-confidence and aloneness. Somehow, in some rock-bottom way I didn't care about the introjected authorities in my mind, the success-ghosts, the lyrics of reward-mongers—I cut through them. But I assumed there would be a worldly reward, a permanent order of recognition, a clear and continuous placement of my work in the critical adumbrations of the establishing world. To live awaredly in that world, no longer envisaging myself as say Emily or Melville in his last 30 dog years, is the outer mandala, the inner and secret ones potential. Fear's part of all mandalas; my fear of being out-there comes from a tactician's pettiness. Awareness of literary politics is not the same as craven submission; since I'm not craven, but thirsty for *la gloire*, I've sometimes elected withdrawal.

How to get to or into or be with the very thing? Which is the only real pleasure. All pleasure with words is a kind of *pis-aller.* – / last resort; final resource)

To produce poetry in order to come closer to, to better understand the nature of suffering. If one is to have an aim, this, which was the Buddha's, will be the workable one. (Wm James's pragmatism as reference).
Form: "The Talmud: an incurable thicket of reeds through which each traveler makes his own path." (—Eban) So literature/legend/law/
teachings/memoirs/laboratory operations/maxims/parables/magic/science

What things are to be learned from Gide's "*Journal des Faux-Monnayeurs*"?

Tablet XXVIII: children, blind/chosen
        storehouse
        Leviticus
        palimpsest, X-Ray
        sacred text
        eating the children

Bridge materials experience fatigue; tensile strength; elongation boundary till skin tear

S/T's anti "Semitism"

Check the nature of the Talmudic thicket

re: Gardiner in *Egyptian Language* : "confusion" between gynecological and veterinary papyri ,from the same place, *Il âhun...* Also comments on many unidentifiable names of drugs and diseases—psychoses in the archaic world?

Omen tablets were sometimes made in the shape of liver-lobes, or birds; (which birds?) To publish hepatoscopic Tablets, avian Tablets in their omen shapes?

S/T to refer to how some ur-language font figures relate ancestrally to Mandelbroit and fractals!?

I'm in a real bind about what to be doing with the Scholar/Translator. Under the spell of Jabès, through Jason Weiss's interview w. Jabès in *Conjunctions* I'm thinking about my situation; dialogue; questions. I can't speak in my "own" voice in *The Tablets*.

To have a *dialogue* with the pictographs and their nature would be a satisfying way to bring up questions, including complex and representative variables in the S/T's character.

The possible use of say "affective" determinatives, as: the thinking within the pain of thinking. (Thinking one of the 6 senses in Buddhist teachings; how far back, and where, might that formulation go?) Feeling-category pointer. The S/T might write brief essays *au fur et à mesure que*....And after a while and some acquaintance the S/T no longer needs to define the determinatives.

Steve Gorn's useful comment: ... "the raga-scale is *there*; the work of improvisation, "whatever that is," exists in the tension between fixity and desire to float away.

Aha: from Walker's British Museum pamphlet on Eblaite: "...80% of the words in the Ebla texts are Sumerian. Interspersed among these Sumerian signs the remaining signs reflect the local language, now called Eblaite. Broadly speaking, most of the nouns, verbs and adjectives occurring in the economic texts are written in Sumerian, and most of the prepositions, pronouns, conjunctions and personal names are written syllabically in Eblaite." A treasure of suggestions.

Use quotes fm. scholars, as e.g. fm. Powell in *Visible Language*, 421, "...an accounting system, the rules of which we do not know and are unlikely ever to recover."

Archaic organizational methods: 1) Clustering small groups of signs. 2) Structuring tablet surface into a regular series of compartments—columns and cases—separated by straight dividing lines.

—M W Green: in *Visible Language*, 349

"In the ancient world, including the great civilizations of Egypt and Mesopotamia, the brain was regarded as an unimportant organ. Thought and the emotions were attributed to the stomach, the liver and the gall bladder.... When the Egyptians embalmed their dead, they did not trouble to keep the brain (which was extracted through the left nostril) though the other organs

[handwritten marginal note:] These were his own working notes collected during the process of his work on the tablets (or so they seem)

146

were separately preserved, in special Canopic jars placed beside the sarcophagus. In death the brain is almost bloodless, so perhaps it seemed ill-suited to be the seat of life, warmth and feeling..."

    —R L Gregory, *Eye and Brain: the Psychology of Seeing*, McGraw Hill, 37

Alexander Marshak: "For almost one year I studied the drawings and photographs of the Ice Age artifacts in the scientific journals, making copies, comparing examples, doing computations, making charts." How close I feel to him decades later! Marshak also says, "At times I felt like a man trying to structure a building with oozing sands of the sea."

How shall I conceive of the post-*XXV Tablets*? It, they're, no longer to be intuited and experienced only, or essentially restrictable through, *Kenosis* and *Plerosis*. Interesting that E.P. called late Cantos "Rock-Drill" and Stevens the last book, "the Rock." "...the pleasure of a pure repose."

XXV →

I have it!! the first *Tablet* in the new mind-world: a blind Tiresias-like figure who is, exceptionally for the culture, in touch with mind-texture (although it isn't clear later in *The Tablets* whether his capability is actually so rare, or whether it's the S/T's conceit) evident

[Thinking his way through the tablets to h... (we have access) thought process) His working notes]

the ruminant-stomach, liver, gall bladder logo./icon....

But how many in the sequence? Remain open? Math? Fibonnaci?

"In the beginning simple words were enough: food; water; life. Both prose and poetry are but an extension of language." —Louis Zukofsky, quoted by Hugh Kenner

... crossroads where biology, philosophy, linguistics ... intersect.] *

Shall I use the O.T. as one grid for *XXVI* and after? Genres/Variants/Mixed linguistic derivations (e.g. J and E and P documents ...)/Source of paradigms?

homo ludens?
homo sapiens?
homo rationalis
homo fodens?   the insensate digger

"A literal rendering of Proverbs 1 6:18 would be something like this:

       before breaking [is] pride
         and before falling [is] haughtiness of mind.

What gives this proverb its punch in Hebrew is a quick juxtaposition of images, an almost stroboscopic effect... a rapid flash of words...The New English Bible is accurate enough, but it practically turns the proverb into pale prose:

Pride comes before disaster

Here all the vividness, the picturing power of the proverb, is lost."
—Alter and Kermode

To include cognate madnesses into *XXVI*, in this case the U. of Penn. *Sumerian Dictionary*, which hasn't got a single utterance, syllable, in cuneiform. A kind of rape.

"The Center is everywhere": *Eastern Buddhist*, XX, 1, 52

Tablets : like Finnegans Wake, a drama w. *timings*—inside a meditation *XXVI* and O.T. Genesis

Really go into a tale, a "fact"—then the nausée (for the reader) of yawning gap, language construct that it helplessly is

S/T lets reader in to translation process. The reader must be told the almost-truth most *determinedly* and almost totally. S/T: secret agenda?

O.T. paradigm: *Tablets* I see now, I have another model. "not a book at all, in the usual sense of the term, but an anthology—a set of selections from a library of religious and nationalistic writings produced over a period of some one thousand years." "style" "point of view" "message"

Check Cortasar's *Hopscotch* for undecidabilities

get that M/T/D Blocker in there!

... an appearance of unity results at times when the Bible quotes or derives something from itself, such as when the N.T. brings in "prophecies" from the O.T. to make a Christian case. Cf. "suffering servant" as later Messiah. Uses of power in historical record-makings. The winners....
?Plant language through pictographs?

S/T *XXVII*: The pictograph for ⚚ ⌇ ⌣ ⅃ ✻ ⫷ weighs seven times as much as its equivalent cuneiform

S/T puts together different pictographs/& combos of pictos and cuneiforms in particular kinds of containing boxes. How will S/T present collocations of historically disjunct writing systems? It's the ease of access to both fonts which breeds the idea, which then generates questions about language change etc. And then:

Different kinds of bounds—joined expressions need music [?] to be performed, to ease, or overcome, or celebrate or mourn the [neologism] which I originally called Synerjects. The S/T found the name Ominacunei apt. Thus the comments on the cylinder seals partake of the electro-verbals (E-E.V world) which preoccupy the S/T at the end of *XXVII*.

More "musical" notation: a determinative which governs the passage of an utterance from one body into another. Another sign: that of freezing isolation, the reciprocal of which is compassion.
Or, "the second spontaneity," as it is found described in one of the first cuneiform descriptions of the oral performer's art, or to use a probably more precise rendition, the performer's *trimming*.

Signs: WEIGHT
　　　SHAPE (e.g. to be chanted as a triangle)
　　　THICKNESS (e.g. to be uttered while conceiving of oneself as the average width of a pale, inscribed rectangle of shaved bone

Laboratory Teachings Memoirs: Laboratory—collecting, observing
　　　　　　　　　　　　　Teachings—hermeneutics
　　　　　　　　　　　　　Memoirs—the experiential
　　　Trouble is these don't really include the initiatory: *dialogue*, eventuating in education and exegesis. (cf. Clifford)

The mystery of the bounds around utterances: say like botanical gardens, zoos, historic sites ... all "wrapped". What remains unwrapped? Illimitability ... Paleolithic man? Throat angle and tongue and larynx setting: speech? Idea: certain wrappings to make some utterances invulnerable to Time. Permawrap. Something at the end of *XXVII*.

Other signs: Note Marcel Griaule's comments on looking down on anthropological site from an airplane: thus, approach scape of utterance; from what physical position a reader actually engages an utterance; the role of 3-dimensional imagination. For instance: standing, seated, crouching, giving birth, crouched dying. ...

investigating our reception of language (what we normally take for granted)

Find within the Mind/Texture/Determinative icons overlays, palimpsest : earlier recoverable layer of divinatory modes

check "stratus" "stratigraphy" in Unabridged. Stratigram and pictograph give:
density

vert and horiz

Some further explanation of the significance of M/T/D?

Sound aspects of M/T/D'S? including notations relating to, say, waver or trill or ulu-
lation or yodel or gargling utterance(s)

M/T/D 3X size along w. utterance might = a headache, a painful disjunction implic-
it in the utterance and the body of the utterer: such was the assumption of order and
shared certainties that commonly agreed-upon matrices of psychic pains or delights
could be linguistically, graphically, denoted.

Say 6x = migraine

12x = terminal disease. or how to establish

different
white on black

densities of signs, perhaps

Some M/T/D's may turn an entire expression of whatever voice into the instant
intransitive
Empty M/T/D =Full one?!

Generate more pictofonts: models of hiero, domestic, architectural, animal, plant, min-
eral, human...

USE M/T/D'S WITH MY, AMERICAN, TONGUE.

Make a continually evolving CHART for my reference and triggering electricity of
the various denotations and connotations of the M/T/D world. Check Blake Urizen,
others

Work through, and deceive, my expectation, disown the experience. Then the space
is pregnant

"kalit birkim": "kidney of the penis" (scrotum?)

"...not a liver but a lung..."

"...the behavior of the sacrificial lamb when slaughtered is considered as predictive of
future events": cf Hua Yen Buddhism, net of Indra totalities/holographic universe

"To make visible how the world touches us." Merleau-Ponty on Cézanne

150

M/T/D modes:
    Condensing
    Compound
    Mixture   of pictographs

    Held in solution in another

    Magnetizing pictos

Panic may generate a word, language, an uncontrollable need to fill the palpable emptiness which, at precisely the same instant, generates the sounds of its own name(s)

Use of, w. examples, the M/T/D of e.g. Total Emptiness/Total Interpenetration, or an M/T/D of relative emptiness.

How the way we come to occurrences alters their beings.

I've often found myself confused: the differences between organic and imposed forms, so crucial to poets ... That is, pace *Bibliographia Literaria*, is organic form like a mango drawing its own form, lovely sounding, magical mystery tourist and is imposed form an Iron Maiden? O look at all the little holes; or Look at these tube-worms popping up guided by their own sense of distance from each other! The question is: Meaning, the great avid pursuer; eat it, reject it, shatter it, clobber it, destruct it; no matter, the great conundrum of space, aloneness and suffering

XXVI, like *I*, to manifest many modes. A kind of preliminary fount

Use Aarvo Pärt's *Fratres* as a guide? : repetition with textural alterations and chordal changes, but essentially similar mathematical structure... the use of the distant drumbeats... I'm very open to such musical analogies to poetic structure. The gist like a fine fume escaping leads to compositional developments in the poem and partly leads to the old problem of am I inventing or finding? well, OK

Make a chart of the O.T. Masoretic texts as partial ground for *XXVI* and on. What kind of paradigmatic sense does it make. Genesis input into *XXVI*.

It's humor, and not only, which allows, in the heart of Stevens's meditations, the dramatic, the relational and the confrontational;

Plants and animals have breath. A plant-language w. translatable morphemes bits are beautiful

link tends to become locus

Born from Emptiness, manifesting in different textures, in form with software
buttons for different depths (see Benjamin on Proust) not merely recall through
olfactory accident but levels of consciousness traveled through and traveling in
the self, in a ground of yin/yang animal, vegetable, mineral life. expansion and
contraction of world, matter / anti-matter. Various modes:
>   one clicking different depths
>   one splitting to 2
>   one to the many
>   many to the one

audacity and absurdity: all hot and high after skipping lunch to continue sit-
ting, I said to Sensei at daisan:

Anecdotes

>   MU

how wonderful I am!
my empty body
so fortunately human
is full of stars
the breaths
are counting themselves

He thought for about 20 seconds: "Why limit yourself?" he said.

Important: different "languages," apparent searches—archaeological, ethnolog-
ical, mammalogical etc. mineralogical. All are level, not hieratic or hierarchi-
cal; ambiguous. Only the appearance of diggers' search

interpretations based on scribal reversals: kefesh/shefek. Scribe hears it wrong,
or sees it wrong & copying mistakes.

Ancient Near-Eastern criminal law: principle of compensation: some exchange
of value equalization between person and goods. Biblical criminal law: imper-
missibility of exchange between goods and persons

Looking back at the notes for *XXVI*: after I finished *Tablet I*, having laid down
[I think of *Inferno* Canto I ...] some formal matrices serving as paradigms for
a lot of the rest, *II-V* came—each more or less the embodiment of a single con-
ception, and each much shorter than the first Tablet.

The activity of *XXVI* somewhat parallels the nature of *I*.

But the demands of *XXVII*, in both scope and length, are massive; I see it as with a *XXVI* charge. In the latter I proceeded from the pictographs to the poems, referring to the print-out of the pictographic font.

Now I'm considering already established font-sources for the icons of the Utterance-Texture-Indicators. Either 1. I accept this referential system or 2. I incorporate the U/T/I icons into a font family. In either case I need to be clear about the provenance of the new determinatives; do they appear—"translated" or "transcribed"—in the original notations/language (that includes the S/T's self-confessed "stylizations: of original notations)? Yes. The S/T's parallel notational contributions can be made in white on black using Old Sabaean font, Neon, Estrangela, Mobile—some of which seem to have a slightly comic side. Glossary needed.

In *XXVI*, as I recall, from the first word the S/T's head already entertained the jostling crowd of pictographic icons; I worked through him in the context of these considerations. So the writing of the Tablet, however referred to variously placed notes, proceeded fairly directly. Much of the S/T's commentary has already been written, mightily complicating the work. (Perhaps *XXVIII* shd start with the original text, all or most commentary to follow that composition.) It's true though that in my favorite poem-section of *XXVI* Saggs's book on Babylon was a direct influence.

I must reference a short glossary of the meanings of various boxes which the S/T uses to surround utterances: do I want the reader to be easily able to distinguish among, say,

> M/T/D
> pictograph
> U/T/I
> Cylinder-Seal Language: Ominacunei

these on cylinder-seals I-V.

Seed-words from esoteric *Tablet IX* as possible base for Cylinder-Seal *Tablet, XXVII*:

terror	damp lips of speech surrendered
afflict	earwax
fire	eye-sockets emptied
penis	ground-down fingertips
blood	sacrifice
mouth	pity
foxglove	slow death
owl	dumb
jellyfish	shrinking
sperm	
tears	
pus	
piss	
sweat	
shit	

Speculation about as yet unwritten Esoteric-IX, in case it shows up: What might/would be the esoteric nature of such a Tablet? Addressed to and existing within groupings of initiates. Self-denudations for purposes of ritual findings; the utilization of secret language(s); the discipline of undoing psycho-sexually motivated obstacles ... toward intergender friendship...

On occasion, the S/T will present a kind of Zukofsky/Catullus sound translation

The old in the new: In the Labat book (which lists all Akkadian cuneiform utterances in all developmental forms), the editor writes, "...the language in the predictive [Akkadian] texts differs from that in current Akkadian use. The reader meets ... archaic survivals." René Labat, *Manuel D'Épigraphie Akkadienne, Signes, Syllabaire, Idéogrammes*, 5ème édition, Paris: Librairie Orientaliste Paul Geuthner, S.A., 1976.

Discussion of *sibylline graphics* for esoteric texts in Labat: ... "in order to make texts unavailable to individuals outside the group, the insider chose signs which at the time were so artificial that they could not be accepted as authentically within the Assyrio-Babylonian syllabary." Such "confusions" to leak into Cylinder seal 2. *XXVII*.

Labat: "...certain scribes used a determinative complement in the very interior of a word, in order to facilitate the reading of a syllable the nature of which seemed to them ambiguous." Say "gymphastic," for instance, where *ph* is a suspect phoneme or an oddly shaped cuneiform segment to be corrected to, for instance "gymbodyflexastics."

Postpositional determinatives of plurality, duality, totality etc. were used in Sumerian; Akkadian on the other hand, which is inflected, did not really require these; but concerned with precision the majority of Akkadian scribes included them. Say for instance, in a text concerned with burial ritual the Akkadian word for catafalque, the Akkadian scribe might keep the postpositional determinative *plonz*, the death god; thus: *catafalquaplonz*, even though the context is quite unambiguous .... Interesting possibilities for creating neologisms, perhaps, further, nonsense-holding meaningfulnesses, as in some of Michaux, Lewis Carroll.

Is the intent of the Utterance/Texture/Indicators (U/T/I's) to clarify or to mask the original, more forthrightly expressed, esotericism of the cylinder seals in *XXVII*. (Dealing with the alternative crypto-IX here? The S/T probably intense about the general loss of image, but not sure whether the Seals do or don't illustrate the process.

The survival of the cuneiform for thousands of years appears surprising, given the greater ease for reading offered by the development of later, syllabic, scripts in the Ancient Near East. (The S/T is infuriated by the alphabet.) Labat: "Texts destined to be read by contemporary Akkadians, notably those indebted to Sumerian tradition, proceed from an early, rich primitivism ("...*une idéographie primitivement riche*") to a phonetic system which leaves only a little room for a small number of traditional ideograms; on the other hand, religious, esoteric, divinatory, magic texts, based on more original conceptions, follow an inverse evolution: originally clear, they submit to progressive condensation in the context of an ideology often pushed to extremity."

Labat: "The great literary tablets from Ashur, Nineveh and Uruk feature little holes, either triangular or round. Appearing randomly on the various parts of the tablet, they may occasionally fill one or two entire lines. Most often they seem uniquely destined to decorate any spaces not occupied by writing."

Incunabula—devotional and mystical texts, hagiography, musical printing, fake literature, homiletics, juristics, history and fictionalized history, satire, poetry, romances, travel books, herbals...

Some categories of Akkadian texts:

> Historical
> Religious
> Divinatory (hepatoscopy for instance)
> Letters
> Medical
> Scholarly (lists, commentaries, etc.)
> Legal codes
> Contracts; economic texts (probably most numerous)
> Lists of proper nouns: (people, gods, towns)
> Poetic
> Scientific (mathematical...)
> Colophons
> Bilingual material

Labat: "Akkadians occasionally used pseudo-ideograms, fixed and immutable words or radicals; and crypto-ideograms, artificial sign-groups whose meaning had been arbitrarily fixed; they are rare and are only found in texts set aside for initiates."

Is it useful, interesting, to produce more instances of language-bodies? Let's assume there are in fact no more influences or masters for me. Or since that's by spiritual acculturation impossible, let's assume that I rid my head of previously acknowledged masters. Then what? Nature of greed, freedom, power.

"It is characteristic of unconscious thought to rely on sensory (particularly visual and auditory) projections as means of achieving gratification." Kaja Silverman, *The Subject of Semiotics.*

The M/T/D's sometimes refer to states-of-being whose hidden idiosyncratic natures beg for recognition and often for transformation, lest individuals' life-responses be crippled. Thus M/T/D genesis derives from survival-needs, from the imperative that one see clear, without impediment. (Kant: problem ...)

And the U/T/I , Utterance/Texture/Indicators, constitute in some sense the external social analogues of the M/T/Ds texture and function.

Much interesting poetry now tends to veer towards concerns with dis/ease, avoidance, undoing, backing-and-filling; Simone Weil's "reality of decreation" becomes constrained smallness. The question is: how to attain to relevant largeness...

Dubuffet to Henri Michaux, letter, 13 July 1950, vol. II, 300: "...unlike almost all books yours are not busy generating ideas, nothing but objects, facts, gestures. The other authors are giving speeches; for you, the thing is to *show*."

How not what: as Tarthang Tulku on vajrayana deities—ways of being not things.

"...as Heidegger's etymological discussions on Greek and German philosophical terms ... help us to see philosophical language in a new and creative way, Dogen Zenji too returns to the basic meanings of Chinese characters and thereby makes seemingly innocuous, traditional passages come alive with profoundly Zen meaning."

Zen Action, Zen Person by Kasulis, 159

If the aim, an aim, is to "open up the repressed gap between word and thing," (Rob Wilson) ... to what end? The Bardo-gap—in between—within life and afterlife requires recognition; the adventures in the disjunctive, are they a "lighting out for the territory" or an escape from the fact that there is nowhere to escape to? Actually, in "lighting out for the territory," the great ultimate discovery comes when it descends upon the experiencer that There = Here; Samsara = Nirvana, depending totally on the experiencer.

The pain I felt when I interrupted a lyric song by any of my unknown archaic speakers by intercalating—or rather by finding necessary the presence of— the S/T's discursive, often apparently irrelevant comments, often wrongheaded inventions which nevertheless brought the reader into a consideration of the essential ambiguities of syntax, grammar and translation, a kind of undependable groundlessness of appearance. I remember part of me would almost agree with a hearer's wish that I omit the S/T's commentary as unnecessarily clotting; I'd almost want to accede. But precisely such ambiguities, left somewhat to integrally radiate, is useful work done. The thing is, I wanted not to separate the song from the entropic world. This *and* that.

On the constant S/T's interruption

Somewhere in my Naranjana poem, ecstasy and meditation; yes, and it's been and it's still what I want. There's no old or new in it as long as I'm in language's changing weathers.

Beethoven's 7th, second movement. Tiny motifs. Notes the same same same same, but what harmonic surround! He was I guess already deaf, or on the way.

How did he disown
the experience so
as to leave fermenting
Space
for composition.
Being, Arriving?

How did he hear what he
listened to, to transcribe
as he was also making it?

Where was the Space?

Where is mine?

With good karma we earn deafness

COMPACT DISC

ARMAND SCHWERNER

SELECTIONS FROM THE TABLETS

Recorded by the author, mid-1990s

1. Tablet II / 5:04

2. Tablet IV / 4:01

3. Tablet VI / 7:18

4. Tablet VII / 5:24

5. Tablet VIII / 8:01

6. Tablet IX / 4:53

7. Tablet X / 0:42

8. Design Tablet / 2:10

9. Tablet XIII / 5:33

10. Tablet XIV / 3:42

11. Tablet XV / 5:01

12. Tablet XVII / 3:54

13. Tablet XVIII / 3:43

14. Tablet XIX / 3:09

15. Tablet XXV / 3:17